SIX
PATHWAYS

to Healthy

Child Development

and

Academic Success

Comer Schools in Action
The 3-Volume Field Guide
Edward T. Joyner, James P. Comer, and Michael Ben-Avie, Editors

---

Six Pathways
to Healthy Child Development and Academic Success:
The Field Guide to Comer Schools in Action
James P. Comer, Edward T. Joyner, and Michael Ben-Avie, Editors

Transforming School Leadership and Management
to Support Student Learning and Development:
The Field Guide to Comer Schools in Action
Edward T. Joyner, Michael Ben-Avie, and James P. Comer, Editors

Dynamic Instructional Leadership
to Support Student Learning and Development:
The Field Guide to Comer Schools in Action
Edward T. Joyner, Michael Ben-Avie, and James P. Comer, Editors

James P. Comer, Edward T. Joyner, and Michael Ben-Avie, Editors

SIX PATHWAYS

to Healthy Child Development and Academic Success

The Field Guide to Comer Schools in Action

CORWIN PRESS
A Sage Publications Company
Thousand Oaks, California

For information:

Corwin Press, Inc.
A Sage Publications Company
2455 Teller Road
Thousand Oaks, California 91320
www.corwinpress.com

Sage Publications Ltd.
1 Oliver's Yard
55 City Road
London EC1Y 1SP
United Kingdom

Sage Publications India Pvt. Ltd.
B-42, Panchsheel Enclave
Post Box 4109
New Delhi 110 017 India

Printed in the United States of America

Library of Congress Cataloging-in-Publication Data

Six pathways to healthy child development and academic success: The field guide to Comer schools in action / [edited] by James P. Comer, Edward T. Joyner, Michael Ben-Avie.
        p. cm.—(Comer schools in action)
Includes bibliographical references and index.
    ISBN 1-4129-0508-7 (cloth)—ISBN 1-4129-0509-5 (pbk.)
    1. Yale School Development Program. 2. Comer, James P. 3. Child development—United States.
4. Home and school—United States. 5. Academic achievement—United States. I. Comer, James P.
II. Joyner, Edward T. III. Ben-Avie, Michael. IV. Title. V. Series.

LB1117.S53 2004
305.231—dc22   2004007194

This book is printed on acid-free paper.

Acquisitions Editor:	Faye Zucker
Editorial Assistant:	Stacy Wagner
Production Editors:	Kate Peterson and Diana Axelsen
Copy Editor:	Kristin Bergstad
Typesetter:	C&M Digitals (P) Ltd.
Indexer:	David Luljak
Cover Designer:	Michael Dubowe
Figure Illustrator:	Mark Saba, Med Media Group, Yale University School of Medicine

For Shirley Comer

Contents

Foreword

James Comer and colleagues at the Yale School Development Program (SDP) have made an enormous difference in schools and school districts across the country over the past three decades. There is a wealth of knowledge, insight, strategies, and lessons contained within the range of experiences of SDP parents, community members, students, teachers, staff, principals, districts, and other leaders. The beauty of the *Comer Schools in Action* set is that its three volumes have now given us access to this wealth of knowledge and ideas in one place. This collection is of inestimable value.

The first book lays the foundation: child development = education. *Six Pathways to Healthy Child Development and Academic Success* establishes the mission and vision. What we have here is a fundamental agenda for social reform.

Dynamic Instructional Leadership to Support Student Learning and Development then shows the Comer Process in action, making it clear that we are talking about systemic reform. The elements of reform are clearly set forth: the role of schools and districts, the need for integrated planning and curriculum, the careful focus on implementation, how teamwork drives and sustains change, how school-university partnerships can be developed, and how assertive achievement-oriented leadership at the school and district levels is a system responsibility.

The third book, *Transforming School Leadership and Management to Support Student Learning and Development*, represents a complete guide for how to introduce and carry out the Comer Process. It shows us what is involved in making initial decisions, how to proceed through six essential steps in the planning process, and how to start and continue assessment and monitoring. All the key relationships are addressed, both inside and outside the school. An important chapter sets out the SDP implementation cycle chronologically, taking us through timelines and activities for planning, foundation building, transformation, institutionalization, and renewal.

All in all, the *Comer Schools in Action* trilogy gives us the entire essence of Comer's success and the lessons learned along the way. It is theoretical, practical, and filled with ideas and guidelines for action that integrate theory and practice. The Comer trilogy is a landmark contribution to the field of educational change.

—Michael Fullan
University of Toronto

Preface

This field guide and its two companion books in the *Comer Schools in Action: The 3-Volume Field Guide* are reflective of the wisdom of Dr. James P. Comer, of the staff at the Yale School Development Program (SDP), and of all the people in the hundreds of schools in communities throughout the United States and abroad who have embraced the Comer Schools movement. This volume is the collective representation of what we have learned from parents, children, teachers, administrators, community leaders, politicians, college professors, clergy, and members of the helping professions.

Because we believe that the practitioner is an expert, we have included the voices of people in the field as well as those in the ivory tower. We are all scholar-activists, and when we combine our efforts, pool our knowledge, and achieve one accord on what we want for our children, we cannot be defeated. We can create schools and communities that foster the development of ethical behavior in young people and challenge them to high academic standards.

Enough data have been collected and analyzed by some of our best education researchers to demonstrate that SDP is tried, tested, and true and that its effectiveness as a comprehensive school reform model meets "the highest standard of evidence" (Borman, Hewes, Overman, & Brown, 2003). This field guide will help you see the program through the eyes of the people who have made it work, as well as the people who designed it and continue to refine it.

This field guide is based on and expanded from training materials that we have field tested for decades. It is the first commercially published field guide by our organization. Because we are constantly searching for more ways to help children and the people who serve them, it will not be the last.

—Edward T. Joyner, Ed.D.
Executive Director, School Development Program

REFERENCE

Borman, G. D., Hewes, G. M., Overman, L. T., & Brown, S. (2003). Comprehensive school reform and student achievement: A meta-analysis. *Review of Educational Research, 73*(2), 125–230.

Acknowledgments

We extend our deepest appreciation to the district facilitators, superintendents, principals, school staff, parents, and students within the SDP network. We could not possibly list every individual who contributed to the success of SDP over the past 35 years. In *Dynamic Instructional Leadership to Support Student Learning and Development*, we acknowledge the winners of the Patrick Francis Daly Memorial Award for Excellence in Educational Leadership. In *Transforming School Leadership and Management to Support Student Learning and Development*, we acknowledge by name facilitators and former SDP staff members. In this book, we acknowledge by name superintendents, university partners, board presidents, and staff at state education departments.

Superintendents, Staff at State Education Departments, and Board Presidents

Dr. Arlene Ackerman
Mona Bailey
Dr. Kenneth Burnley
Dr. Karen Campbell
Dr. Eugene Carter
Dr. Evelyn Castro
Dr. Juanita Clay Chambers
Phyllis Chase
Dr. Constance Clark
Dr. Jerome Clark
Dr. Pablo Clausel
Dr. Ramon Cortines
Dr. Eddie Davis
Dennis Deloatch
Yvette Douglas
Dr. John Dow
Dr. Edwin Duroy
Dr. Marvin Edwards
Dr. Barbara Easton-Watkins
Dr. Steve Ernst
Bob Etheridge
Ed Felegy
Constance Frazier
Dr. Libia S. Gil

Cassandra Grant
Dr. E. Jean Harper
Dr. Alice Hart
Dr. James Hawkins
Dr. Lillie Jones
Dr. Mildred Jones
Dr. Charlie-Mae Knight
Dr. Larry Leverett
Dr. Robert Logan
Dr. Reginald Mayo
Patricia McCann-Vissepo
Dr. Peter Mesa
Dr. Iris T. Metts
Dr. John Murphy
Dr. Peter Negroni
Dr. Ralph Nichols
Christopher Owens
Dr. Jacqueline Peek-Davis
Dr. Brian Perkins
Dr. Robert Pinckney
Dr. Columbus Salley
Dr. J. O. Simpson
Dr. Franklin L. Smith
Dr. Steve Stone

Dr. Alvin Thornton
Dr. Gerald Tirozzi
Dr. Bettye Topps
Dr. Carlos Torre
Dr. Edna Vega

Dr. Louise Waynant
Dr. Jerry Weast
Dr. James Williams
Dr. Lester Young

University Partners

Dr. Dan Beach
Dr. Hinsdale Bernard
Dr. Judith Bippert
Dr. Norma Davila
Dr. Robert Dunwell
Dr. Victoria Chou
Dr. Thomas B. Cook
Dr. Gloria Dye
Dr. Barbara Ford
Dr. Alison Harmon
Dr. Diane Harris
Dr. Patty J. Horn
Dr. Sylvia Johnson
Dr. Louise Kaltenbaugh
Dr. Jeffrey Kane
Dr. Kimberly Kinsler
Dr. Nancy Klein
Dr. Rodney Lane
Dr. Carol Malloy
Dr. William Malloy

Dr. Shirley Malone-Fenner
Dr. Robert Mannheimer
Dr. Nora Martin
Dr. Cheryl Mills
Dr. John Moore
Dr. George Noblit
Dr. Charles Payne
Dr. Matthew Proctor
Dr. Jerry Robbins
Dr. Francis Roberts
Regent Adelaide Sanford
Dr. Deborah Smith
Dr. Marilyn Hill Stepney
Dr. Jill McLean Taylor
Dr. Sheila Evans-Tranum
Dr. Betty Vega
Dr. Carol West
Dr. Martha Watson
Dr. Jayne White

We would like to acknowledge the kindness and generosity of various philanthropic organizations that have supported our work over the years, including

Carnegie Foundation
Community Trust (Chicago)
DeWitt-Wallace Foundation
Ford Foundation
MacArthur Foundation
Melville Corporation

Polk Brothers Foundation (Chicago)
Rockefeller Foundation
San Francisco Foundation
The Skillman Foundation
U.S. Department of Education

Without their support we could not have achieved as much as we have in recent years.

We extend our gratitude and admiration to the SDP copyediting and proofreading team of Linda Brouard, Beverly Crowther, and Eva Stein.

Publisher's Acknowledgments

Corwin Press extends its thanks to the following reviewers for their contributions to this work:

Michelle Barnea, Educational Consultant, Millburn, NJ

Dominic Belmonte, Golden Apple Foundation for Excellence in Teaching, Chicago, IL

Jo Ann Canales, Texas A & M University, Corpus Christi, TX

Robert Ricken, Educational Consultant, Lido Beach, NY

Mary M. Williams, University of San Diego, CA

About the Authors

Virginia Arrington is assistant superintendent for special education, Community School District 17, New York City Department of Education. She is interested in ensuring that each student with a disability receives an appropriate individualized education program in the least restrictive environment consistent with that student's needs.

Michael Ben-Avie, Ph.D., directs the Impact Analysis and Strategies Group, which studies corporate, nonprofit, and government partnerships that promote youth development and student learning. He conducts national studies designed to evaluate the effectiveness of mentoring programs and psychological interventions on children's lifepaths. Dr. Ben-Avie has coedited books about the Yale School Development Program with James P. Comer, M.D., and colleagues, and has published numerous book chapters, articles, and reports on educational change initiatives, high schools, parent involvement, and the relationship between youth development and student learning.

Fay E. Brown, Ph.D., is an associate research scientist at the Yale Child Study Center. She is the director of Child and Adolescent Development and the director of the Essentials of Literacy Process for the School Development Program. Her major focus is on helping schools create and maintain developmentally appropriate conditions to ensure the holistic development of every child.

James P. Comer, M.D., is the founder and chairman of the Yale School Development Program, Maurice Falk Professor of Child Psychiatry at the Yale Child Study Center, and Associate Dean of the Yale University School of Medicine. He has published seven books, more than 35 chapters, over 400 articles in popular journals, and more than 100 articles in professional journals. He has served as a consultant, committee member, advisory board member, and trustee to numerous local, national, and international organizations serving children and youth. Dr. Comer has been the recipient of the John and Mary Markle Scholar in Academic Medicine Award, the Rockefeller Public Service Award, the Harold W. McGraw, Jr. Prize in Education, the Charles A. Dana Award for Pioneering Achievement in Education, the Heinz Award for Service to Humanity, and many other awards and honors, including 41 honorary degrees.

Joanne N. Corbin, Ph.D., is an epidemiologist and social worker. She is an associate professor at the Smith College School of Social Work. Her research focuses on social workers as change agents in school reform.

Shalewa Crowe, M.Ed., is a member of the Youth Guidance team of Comer facilitators serving Chicago elementary schools. She is a former administrator and teacher in a private Afrocentric elementary school, and a trained reading specialist. She believes that schools must be structured so that students can be taught in a supportive, engaging environment that encourages risk taking and decision making.

Everol Ennis, M.Ed., is a School Development Program implementation coordinator with a background in counseling psychology. He serves as the intake coordinator for SDP and is the director of the Youth Development Unit, which oversees the Comer Kids' Leadership Academy. He is interested in issues relating to effective teaming and problem solving. In addition, he is involved in various community and civic organizations whose goals are to impact the lives of youths.

Morton Frank, Ph.D., is supervisor of school psychologists, Community School District 17, New York City Department of Education. He is interested in the use of home-school collaboration meetings for students with conduct problems.

Jeffery German is an implementation coordinator with the School Development Program. He was principal of a Comer middle school in the Guilford County Public Schools that won several awards for notable achievement. He is a past winner of the Patrick Francis Daly Memorial Award for Excellence in Educational Leadership.

Carmen S. Gonzalez is principal of the Edward C. Blum Elementary School (P.S. 46) in Brooklyn, New York. In 2001, she received the Patrick Francis Daly Memorial Award for Excellence in Educational Leadership and the New York City Board of Education 2001 Outstanding Educator Award.

Alice Huff Hart, Ed.D., recently retired as associate superintendent for curriculum and instruction for Asheville City Schools. During her 37 years as an educator, she received numerous awards, including 1985 North Carolina Principal of the Year. She designed and edited a book, *Journeys in Education Leadership*, that contains essays on leadership by 17 North Carolina Principals of the Year. In 1997 she wrote *Seminar Teaching: Five Case Studies* for the Principals' Executive Program in Chapel Hill, North Carolina.

Fred Hernández, Ed.D., is currently principal of the Commerce Middle School in Yonkers, New York. He successfully used the SDP model to remove an elementary school from the NYSED "SURR" process. He led a high school with SDP principles and mechanisms to strategically represent the school as an "authentic workplace" for students to experience academic success. In 1998 he was honored with the Patrick Francis Daly Memorial Award for Excellence in Educational Leadership.

J. Patrick Howley, C.A.G.S., is the director of Teachers Helping Teachers and an implementation coordinator who specializes in human relations work such as team building, communication, and conflict resolution. He has been with the School Development Program for 13 years.

Edward T. Joyner, Ed.D., is the executive director of the Yale School Development Program. He served as SDP's first director of training, was the original designer of the SDP leadership development academies, and initiated university-public school partnerships to strengthen local school reform efforts. He is the architect of SDP's systemic initiative, which coordinates the work of the school board, central office, building staff, and the larger school community to create an optimal environment for teaching and learning throughout the school district. He currently oversees all of the operations of SDP and serves as the lead implementation coordinator for New York.

Valerie Maholmes, Ph.D., has worked at the School Development Program for 10 years and is currently director of research and policy. Her areas of interest include examining the impact of school and classroom context on teachers' and students' sense of efficacy. She has served on the Board of Education for New Haven Public Schools and as chair of its Curriculum Committee.

Nora Martin, Ph.D., is professor at Eastern Michigan University and EMU coordinator for the Comer Schools and Families Initiative. She has been a professor in special education since 1967. Her areas of specialization include parental involvement and learning styles. She is an implementation consultant to the School Development Program.

Miriam McLaughlin is an implementation coordinator for the School Development Program in North Carolina and South Carolina. Her areas of specialization include resiliency, parent involvement, and working with groups. She is the coauthor of a number of books and articles on health and education processes.

Robert A. Murphy, Ph.D., is a clinical psychologist who serves as research coordinator for the National Center for Children Exposed to Violence at the Yale Child Study Center. His research is focused on community intervention for children affected by violence and trauma, as well as evaluation of community programs related to child trauma and other forms of adversity.

Grace Nebb is currently the principal of Avocado Elementary School in Miami-Dade County and a member of the district Comer Action Team. She was principal of Fienberg/Fisher Elementary School from 1992 through 1999. In 1995, she received a Patrick Francis Daly Memorial Award for Excellence in Educational Leadership.

Robert Raymond is chairperson, Community School District 17, New York City Department of Education. He is interested in creating a school environment in which all students (including limited English proficient/English language learners/students with special needs) have equal access to the same quality programs and services.

Jan Stocklinski has dedicated over 18 years to the Comer School Development Program. She is currently a senior implementation coordinator. From 1985 to retirement in 2000, she directed the Comer office of Prince George's County Public Schools in Maryland, where she served a total of 32 years. Her professional interests include school reform, parent and family involvement, child and adolescent growth and development, teaming, and effective practices, including effective use of communication skills. For 16 years she taught part-time in the graduate program at Western Maryland College (recently renamed McDaniel University).

Part I

Child Development = Education

1

The School
Is Preventive
and Promotive

James P. Comer

Well-functioning schools challenge students with developmentally appropriate tasks that help them gain essential skills, behaviors, and ways of understanding the world that they will need to develop into well-functioning adults. To explain the relationship of children's growth and development to their success in school and in later life, child psychiatrist and founder of the School Development Program (SDP) James P. Comer employs four key principles: (1) Children are immersed in their social networks; (2) a child from a poorly functioning family is more likely to enter school without adequate preparation; (3) healthy development along all of the six developmental pathways prepares children to meet life's tasks; and (4) the school is a continuous presence in the lives of children and adolescents. Schools that use the SDP model function as a portal through which the potential benefits of the larger society enter children's daily school and family life, and through which the children and their families emerge to participate fully in the larger society.

A poor school experience interferes with academic achievement and leads to psychological, social, and behavioral problems. In contrast, a good school experience can prevent school failure and promote students' chances of being successful in life. Well-functioning schools expose students to a variety of ideas and challenge them with developmentally appropriate tasks. These schools produce students who gain essential skills, knowledge, habits, attitudes, behaviors, ways of approaching problems, and ways of understanding the world that they will be able to rely on in order to develop into well-functioning adults.

People ask me why we have to promote these qualities in children: "Why won't children develop them on their own?" I answer that there are multiple forces at play in the life of a child. Some are negative and some are positive. Children are not born with the capacity to distinguish between them, nor are they necessarily influenced by the positive. Therefore all the adults around them—in their family, their community, and their schools—should be involved in the process of helping them avoid the negative and adopt the positive.

People also ask me: "Is this the role of schools?" I answer that the mission of the school is to prepare people to be successful in school and in life. Whether in school, or in life in general, you need more than preparation for academic success. You need to begin to know (1) how to get along with other people, (2) how not to be victimized by others, (3) how to solve problems without compromising the rights and needs of other people, and (4) how to establish habits that are going to be useful in moving you toward success in the world and that enable you to meet your life tasks and responsibilities. Because all of these skills are necessary, the school limits its own opportunity to be successful when it focuses only on academic material.

The federal government's involvement in education is based on the general welfare clause of the Constitution. The school is the most effective leverage point to help children grow in ways that are in the best interest of themselves, their families, their communities, and in turn, the larger society. Schools shouldn't have to do it all, but given the fact that we have allowed communities to decline, we can use the school as an institution that can help regenerate the vitality of communities and help students grow.

When I say that schools have a preventive and promotive role, I'm speaking primarily of their role in relation to the children. The people working in the institutions around the children are important because the children are influenced by them and can internalize their attitudes, values, and ways of functioning in the world. They will continue to need helpful people and institutions around them all the way along their journey toward maturation.

There is another important point: The way we traditionally use schools is very wasteful. We limit a myriad of adults to 20 percent of what they could do. The other 80 percent of what is possible would be to help children develop and become successful citizens. Countries whose schools have a real focus on development are getting much more out of their workforce.

To illustrate the relationship of children's growth and development to their success in school and in later life, I have developed a four-panel poster titled "The School Is Preventive and Promotive" (Figures 1.1–1.4). This chapter discusses each of those panels.

CHILDREN ARE IMMERSED IN THEIR SOCIAL NETWORKS

In Panel 1 of the poster (Figure 1.1), I show that children are nurtured in nested environments, depicted as platforms of increasing size. I call the central platform the

Figure 1.1 Children are immersed in their social networks

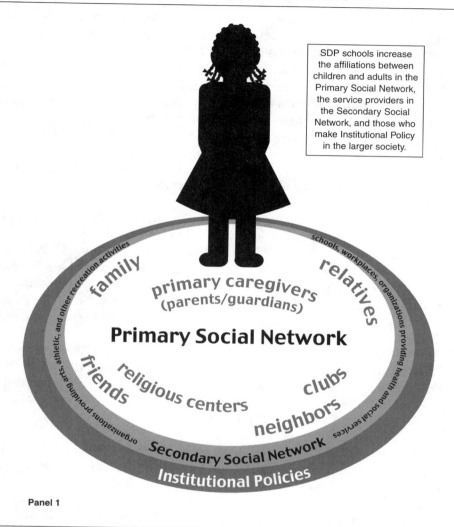

SDP schools increase the affiliations between children and adults in the Primary Social Network, the service providers in the Secondary Social Network, and those who make Institutional Policy in the larger society.

Panel 1

"Primary Social Network," which includes primary caregivers (parents, guardians); immediate family and close relatives; and significant groups such as religious centers, clubs, and friends and neighbors of the family. These groups are those to which the primary caregivers and children feel a sense of belonging. The parents and guardians are the carriers of the attitudes, habits, values, and ways of this Primary Social Network, and they pass them on to the children.

In a complex society like ours, the platform outside the Primary Social Network is what I call the "Secondary Social Network." Organizations in this network provide arts, athletics, and other recreational activities. Included in this network are schools, workplaces, and organizations providing health and social services. Within the Secondary Social Network are all of the organizations that provide the essential services that families need in order to function in the society. The workplace—the job—is a very special kind of essential service because a job, or source of income, is necessary in order to afford all of the other services.

Families may or may not feel that they are a part of the network of service and community organizations. Children from families that feel that they belong in and would like to be in the mainstream of American society are more often prepared to elicit support and respect from the mainstream of society. They feel the school is their school. It's there for them. However, many families are marginalized by societal messages that suggest they're not valued people. Children from these families sometimes do not view the school as their place. Their parents may feel the same way in the workplace and the other places that they go, and transmit to their children this feeling of being marginalized and unimportant.

But in school as in psychotherapy, the people and the environment are part of the instrumentation of learning and development. Therefore the classroom teacher must create the conditions in which the child feels that he or she belongs. Teachers must make an emotional attachment to the children and the children have to make an emotional attachment to the teachers because that's what makes it possible for the child to *imitate, identify with, and internalize* the attitudes of the best teacher and the best school people. Without that emotional contact there may be rejection, ambivalence, or a reluctance to get involved.

The School Development Program (SDP) increases opportunities for these emotional connections by increasing the quantity and quality of affiliations between the children and adults who are in the Primary Social Network, and the adults who provide services in the Secondary Social Network. In effect, SDP moves the school from its position in the Secondary Social Network into a close, positive attachment with the child's Primary Social Network.

I call the platform outside the Secondary Social Network, "Institutional Policies." These are the operating rules, procedures, and actions taken by government, business, and organizations in the larger society. These policies and actions can also be preventive and promotive, but unfortunately, what they prevent and promote is not always in the best interest of the healthy development and life success of all children.

SDP schools and school systems try to influence institutional policies at all levels. In this way they are a continual reminder to those who do not usually spend time in schools that children's well-being should in some way be a central concern of all public and private institutions. Furthermore, through school activities that prepare students for community involvement, children and adults in SDP schools develop essential habits of involved citizenship. It is SDP's vision of the future that many of these students will someday directly influence institutional policies as they work in civil service, hold elected positions in government, and become leaders of private industry.

SDP connects strongly to the Primary Social Network, partners with other institutions in the Secondary Social Network, and continually seeks to partner with and influence those who establish institutional policies. In this way, SDP models a portal through which potential benefits of the larger society enter the children's daily school and family life, and through which the children and their families emerge to participate fully in the larger society.

CHILDREN FROM POORLY FUNCTIONING FAMILIES ARE LIKELY TO ENTER SCHOOL WITHOUT ADEQUATE PREPARATION

Families that experience themselves in the mainstream of society feel that they belong. Families that experience rejection and not being valued receive the message that they are expected to remain where they are—at the margins of society—regardless of their talents.

There is a third category of families as shown in Panel 2 (Figure 1.2): Antisocial children and families who feel so undervalued and unwanted that they cannot identify with mainstream attitudes, habits, values, and mores. Children in this category begin to act out in a manner that traps them in antisocial activities and ways of life. Their values and behaviors are going to get them into very grave trouble as they interact with the mainstream. Children who come from moderately functioning families can be pulled into this antisocial group or they can be pulled into the mainstream. The school has a responsibility to give everyone an opportunity to participate in the mainstream.

Unfortunately, we can already identify the "winners" and "losers" in kindergarten. The losers are the children who are acting up and acting out. They can't sit still. They can't identify with the attitudes, habits, values, and ways that are going to lead to successful performance and opportunities for success in life. Even in poorly functioning schools, some of those children will have positive developmental experiences in school. Maybe some will turn out to be athletically gifted or musically gifted or have some other talent. They may break into a mainstream pattern that gives them an opportunity because of that talent. But even though they enter the mainstream, they may not be able to sustain themselves there. They may "self-destruct" because they do not develop in ways that allow them to make the most of their mainstream opportunities.

Children elicit positive or negative responses. The winners have been taught how to behave by their parents and their caretakers. For example, at a park my two-year-old granddaughter got on a slide, and a little boy was in her way. The children had been told at the nursery school to politely tell their friends: "You're in my space; please get out of my space." Being really upset with the boy, she said in a pushy manner, "You're in my space!" And she was really upset with him. Her mother told her, "No, Nicole. It's his turn to be in that space now." Nicole is fortunate in that she has many adults giving her instruction about how to handle situations, and also helping her practice. When her behavior is inappropriate, her mother and the other adults help her correct it. That is what mainstream children receive.

Teachers need to understand that they can interact with children from families that are not functioning well in ways that will give the children the capacity to improve their chances of being successful in school and in the world. When children are behaving in ways that will get them in trouble, teachers can interrupt the pattern by providing them with alternative ways to respond. Having children examine the decisions they make will help children previously destined to become losers have a chance to become winners and to make it in the world.

Figure 1.2 Children from poorly functioning families are likely to enter school without adequate preparation

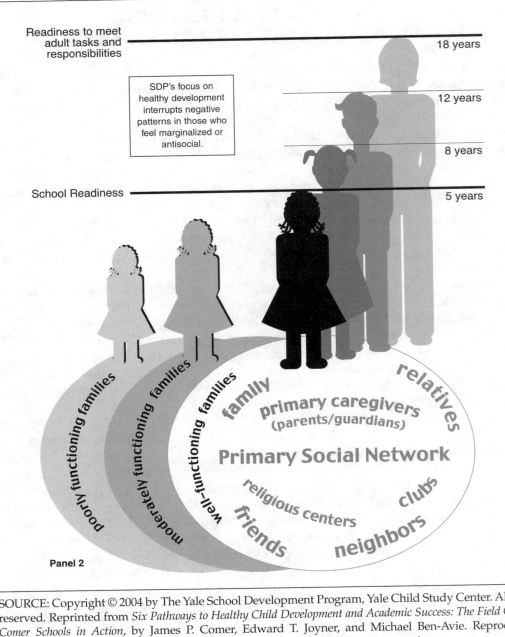

Panel 2

All children elicit positive, apathetic, or negative feelings and behaviors from their caretakers and those around them. Children who display desirable behaviors reinforce their teachers' continued positive response. If they display apathetic or negative behavior, they reinforce their teachers' response in apathetic or negative ways. The opposite is also true: The teachers' positive, apathetic, or negative feelings and behaviors can trigger the children's response. For example, as a school superintendent, my brother used to stand at the door and find one positive thing to say to each child, even to the most troubled child. Then, the teachers tried it. They came back to my brother and told him that even difficult children smiled or touched them. The kids were "looking up" all day because of their positive attachment with the teacher. This positive connection is often like an oasis in the desert. It's very powerful and very important because that's all the positive feedback some children receive.

SDP provides extensive training so that both adults and children can interrupt these apathetic or negative feelings and behaviors and enter into a healthy cycle of mutually eliciting positive feelings and behaviors from one another. Here's an example of how we got teachers to begin to work this way: A teacher came out of a meeting at which we had talked about not yelling at the kids. Kids were running down the hall, and she started to yell. Then—"Oops!"—she caught herself. The discussion had prompted the interruption of the pattern, but the habit was not there yet. She caught herself. So the next time she could catch herself even earlier—before she yelled. Then she would have changed her pattern.

HEALTHY DEVELOPMENT PREPARES CHILDREN TO MEET LIFE'S TASKS

Panel 3 (Figure 1.3) conveys the essential nature of healthy development and what the school can do to support that development through curriculum and programs. To meet life's tasks, children need precursor experiences, good health and nutrition, a spiritual life, and leisure time activities. Schools that successfully prepare children to meet their adult responsibilities do so by creating a curriculum that is geared to doing all of these things. Successful schools begin preparing children from the first day in kindergarten: How do you make decisions about things? How do you understand? How do you watch for somebody trying to pull the wool over your eyes? (Children need to know how to be wary and yet not feel anxious all the time.) Adults begin teaching children how to think, how to manage their lives, how to be involved in all the institutions in society, and how to manage in those institutions—and this is done throughout their education.

Schools need to prepare children to take care of themselves in the areas of health, nutrition, politics and government, leisure, spiritual activities, and business and economics. We have one of the lowest voting rates in the postindustrial world, and that's disgraceful. Even people who can afford health care and take care of themselves are increasingly becoming obese and have a host of other health problems. There are people who can't handle themselves on the weekend because their lives are not structured, so they get drunk, use drugs, and then pull themselves together to go back to work. People have to be able to handle their leisure time and engage in spiritual activities and other formal and informal activities, but children are not being prepared to take care of themselves.

People ask me whether this is the role of the school. I respond: "Why not the school? And if not the school, who?" People then suggest: "The family." I say that the family needs more help today because the family is no longer in control of all of the information and all the forces that impinge on the child. The child has to manage more by himself or herself. Increasingly, children have to make decisions on their own about what they should do, what they shouldn't do, what they can do, what they're going to do. The family has less influence. The school is there and doesn't

Figure 1.3   Healthy development along all of the six developmental pathways prepares children to meet life's tasks

Panel 3

take advantage of its potential to help the kids and society at large. The more kids are helped to make good, reasonable decisions, the better off the society. The school also is able to provide consistent support: Although some children are homeless, few are school-less.

There are well-functioning families that are able to guide their children. Currently, it's possible that most families are not able to guide their children adequately. Even when the parents are present, in many families the parents don't see guidance as their activity. A woman at a health center told me that she was irritated by the school's wanting her to participate. She said: "I send my kids to school. I don't want to be bothered with that. They should teach them." The school has to challenge that notion and, at the same time, both support the development of the child and help the parent understand that he or she needs to be involved. Children need their parents to support their development and to think of additional ways to continue that development.

Right now many schools do not recognize their role as child developers. They've been told that their job is to give children academic material. There was a time when, if that was all schools did, and the children didn't do too well, it didn't matter that much because the children eventually could go out and get a job in spite of not having a good education. Scientific and technological advances, however, are increasing the level of development needed to succeed. That level is now the highest that has ever been required in the history of the world. We cannot afford to allow so many able children to be unprepared to function well in life. The school has to be more active in creating the conditions that will allow children to be successful in school and in life.

In SDP schools, we encourage teachers to create these conditions by participating in the life of the school and by supporting the development of the children in their classrooms. They serve on the School Planning and Management Team (SPMT) or subcommittees. In the classroom, they are encouraged not to yell at the children, overcontrol them, punish them, or have low expectations of them. They elicit positive responses from the children and teach the children how to elicit positive responses from the adults in their lives.

Parents are the first child developers and teachers, but some must be encouraged to think differently. I talk about three mind-sets of parenting: As the owner of children, as the servant of children, and as the developer of children. If you're the owner, you try to control your kids because you believe that they belong to you. You might think that if you *make* the children do what they're supposed to do, you will have kids who are capable of thinking and of managing themselves. But, it's more likely that they will rebel strongly against you.

Taking on the role of the servant leads to children's troublesome behavior because that role encourages permissiveness: Whatever they want, you let them do it. This does not allow children to develop the skills they will need in order to cope with disappointment and stress, to learn to find substitutes for unacceptable behavior, or to tolerate some frustration in the present while they work to accomplish future goals.

In contrast, when you're the developer of your children, you help them internalize attitudes, habits, values, and ways that lead to academic and life success. You understand that they're not necessarily going to do well in the beginning, that they're a work in progress, and that your job is to help them keep coming back to what they can do and what they can become.

A teacher does the same thing. Basic child development starts with the parent, and then becomes the responsibility of more and more people as the child comes into the school. The coach, or the government teacher, or the choral club director, or print shop teacher must also be a child developer. When I was a student, our print shop teacher said to us one day, "You know, we're not all going to be Albert Einsteins, but we're going to be successful if we take care of our families and develop ourselves as good neighbors and good citizens." They don't even have print shop anymore but those words have stuck with me all my life. He was valuable to me as more than just a print shop teacher because he was an adult in my life who gave me a way of thinking that has been terribly important.

THE SCHOOL IS A CONTINUOUS PRESENCE IN THE LIFE OF CHILDREN AND ADOLESCENTS

When an SDP school is working well, it is a model of a just society. There's growth and learning and success for the adults as well as the children, and no one is left behind. Consensus and collaboration in the positive climate that is supported by the principle of no-fault allows great benefits to flow naturally among the family, school, and community (see Panel 4—Figure 1.4).

The SDP school is a training academy for the rest of life. In order to help students prepare for adult life, the school must actually be reflective of every other aspect of society. Many educators have removed themselves from the world. They have these children over here, and they're pouring information in the general direction of their heads, not asking whether that information has anything to do with what the children are going to be asked to do in life. By way of contrast, SDP provides schools not only with an intellectual focus, but also with a set of logical, progressive steps with which to actually get in there and develop the child's entire being.

I hear new teachers talk about why they go into education. They want to help these poor kids. They want to smother them with love. My response is this: "Don't do that. Care about them, but teach them. Kids aren't born with the capacity of functioning in the world. You have to teach them that. Create caring, but expectant, conditions that will allow them to manage the world as they go out into it."

For example, we want to help children learn how to compete and lose and get up to compete again. One of the lowest income schools in Detroit had the highest fourth-grade test scores in the state. When I visited, they were excited because there was a basketball tournament coming up that they were sure they were going to win. But they lost. The principal told me that she knew they were going to be devastated. How do you make that into a learning opportunity? The next day, at the morning assembly, she talked about how important it is to work as hard as you can to achieve your goals, but that no matter how hard you work sometimes you lose, and you're going to be disappointed. She told them that it's okay to mourn your loss and to feel badly, but then you get over it, get up, and try again. You teach people how to be competitive, how to win graciously and lose graciously, and at the same time, to be determined to try to win tomorrow.

This is a life lesson in self-management: You do the best you can, and when you don't achieve your personal best you are willing and open enough to ask for the help you need. I've seen kids in medical school who almost flunked out because they couldn't ask anybody for help. Successful people are able to look at what is interfering with their successes and are able to deal with it. Teachers must instill the notion that we're not perfect and should not expect perfection of ourselves. We're all just trying to be successful and trying to handle our feelings about not being successful.

Figure 1.4 The school is a continuous presence in the life of children and adolescents

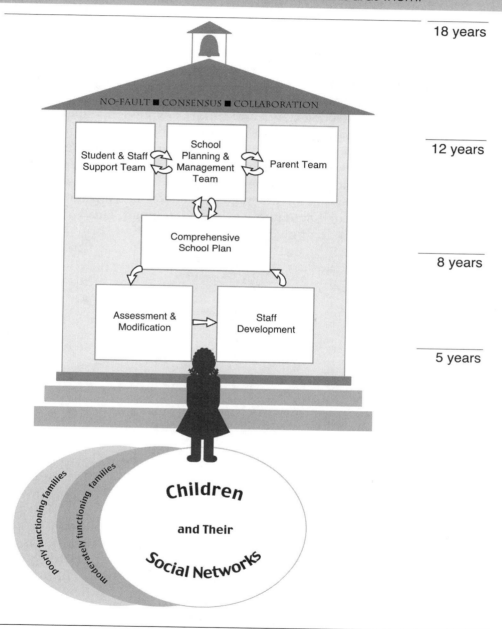

Schools are the only universally accessible institutions in which there are enough adults to foster development along all six pathways. The adults do this by interacting appropriately with children and adolescents and by helping them to manage the information that bombards them.

18 years

12 years

8 years

5 years

Panel 4

In SDP schools the teachers try to instill this notion: Do the best you can, and try to be supportive of each other. At assemblies, if the kids laugh at somebody who is having difficulty, the teachers explain: "You don't laugh. He's doing the best he can do, and you need to help him." And eventually, nobody laughs. But adults must help them behave in this way. Kids who have problems are initially targets of ridicule. But in SDP schools, it is established that it is good to help people who have problems. Students gain a sense of worth and value and confidence by helping others, and then they can also expect others to help them. That makes the whole environment so much safer: knowing that nobody is allowed to be a target. I argue that human beings have a potential for being good and constructive, and bad and destructive. The conditions of the school will determine which one gets favored. We must try to create an environment that brings out and respects that which is good, helpful, and supportive.

When I am feeling down and tired, I acknowledge that and feel it. I am honest with myself about where I am. John Dow, the former superintendent of schools in New Haven, Connecticut, told me that he visited a kindergarten when he felt down and tired. He saw the hopefulness on the faces of the kids, and that helped him. I am determined to help more people understand the importance of child development. When I'm feeling that I'm not making headway and am about to give up, before long I'm back to thinking about how to make it happen. This is deeply rooted in my early experiences: You don't give up.

2

Essential Understandings of the Yale School Development Program

Yale School Development Program Staff

The comprehensive school reform model known as the Comer Process, or Yale University School Development Program (SDP), was established in 1968 as a collaborative effort between New Haven Public Schools and the Yale Child Study Center, an academic research center dedicated to furthering the well-being of children through a clearer understanding of their psychology and growth. More than three decades of research demonstrate that full implementation of the Comer Process leads to high levels of student achievement and development, and that the Comer Process meets the highest standard of evidence of effectiveness. This chapter provides a brief reference guide to the Comer Process.

SDP AND THE COMER PROCESS

The Yale University School Development Program (SDP) is the forerunner of all modern school reform efforts in the United States. In 1968, a Yale Child Study

Center team that was led by James P. Comer, M.D., intervened in two public schools. The team consisted of a social worker, psychologist, special education teacher, and child psychiatrist. The operating system for schools that emerged during those early years in New Haven schools is today fondly known as the Comer Process.

The Comer Process is an educational change initiative based on the principles of child, adolescent, and adult development. It mobilizes teachers, administrators, parents, and other concerned adults to support students' personal, social, and academic growth. It also helps them make better programmatic and curriculum decisions based on students' needs and on developmental principles. The Comer Process is not a project or add-on, but rather an operating system—a way of managing, organizing, coordinating, and integrating activities. SDP practices considered highly controversial in 1969—whole-school change, school-based management, strong parental involvement in decision making, and teacher study groups—are now common in schools throughout the country.

Over the past three decades, our research and the research of others cited throughout this field guide have consistently found that schools that implement the Comer Process at high levels tend to experience high levels of student achievement and development. In general, schools that demonstrate high levels of implementation are those in which adults

- behave in a way that embodies the Comer Process and mind-set
- demonstrate flexibility and expertise in change management
- relate knowledge of child and youth development to student learning
- make decisions that are in the best interests of children

SIX DEVELOPMENTAL PATHWAYS

Of all the prominent educational reformers, only James P. Comer talks about healthy child development as the keystone to academic achievement and life success. Comer uses a metaphor of six developmental pathways to characterize the lines along which children and adolescents mature—physical, cognitive, psychological, language, social, and ethical (see Figure 2.1). In schools using the Comer Process, far more is expected from the students than just cognitive development.

SDP believes that development is the foundation for all learning:

- Child rearing, child development, and learning are inextricably linked.
- Development starts early and must be a continuous process.
- Children's most meaningful learning occurs through positive and supportive relationships with caring and nurturing adults.
- Parents are children's first teachers.
- All parents, staff, and community members, regardless of social or economic status, have an important contribution to make in improving students' education and their preparation for life; therefore, adults must interact collaboratively and sensitively with one another in order to bring out the best in children.

Figure 2.1 The developmental pathways panel

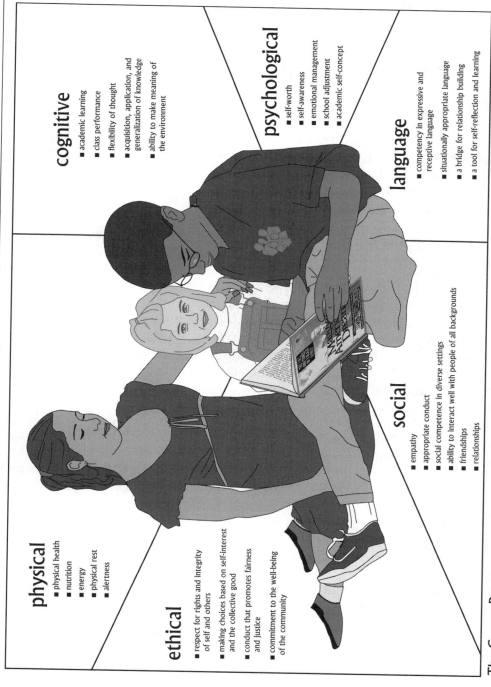

physical
- physical health
- nutrition
- energy
- physical rest
- alertness

cognitive
- academic learning
- class performance
- flexibility of thought
- acquisition, application, and generalization of knowledge
- ability to make meaning of the environment

ethical
- respect for rights and integrity of self and others
- making choices based on self-interest and the collective good
- conduct that promotes fairness and justice
- commitment to the well-being of the community

psychological
- self-worth
- self-awareness
- emotional management
- school adjustment
- academic self-concept

social
- empathy
- appropriate conduct
- social competence in diverse settings
- ability to interact well with people of all backgrounds
- friendships
- relationships

language
- competency in expressive and receptive language
- situationally appropriate language
- a bridge for relationship building
- a tool for self-reflection and learning

The Comer Process promotes growth along all of the six pathways critical to children's learning and development.

SDP is committed to the total development of children and adolescents by helping parents, educators, and policymakers create learning environments that support children's development along the critical pathways. Children who develop well, learn well. Our vision is to help create a just and fair society in which all children have the support for development that will allow them to become positive and successful contributors in family, work, and civic life.

AN OPERATING SYSTEM

The Comer Process provides a structure as well as a process for mobilizing adults to support students' learning and overall development. It is a different way of conceptualizing and working in schools, and it replaces traditional school organization and management with an operating system that works for schools and the students they serve. The schoolhouse graphic in Figures 2.2 and 2.3 displays the nine basic elements of the system.

The following three teams are the hallmark of the Comer Process:

- **School Planning and Management Team:** The SPMT develops a comprehensive school plan; sets academic, social, and community relations goals; and coordinates all school activities, including staff development programs. The team creates critical dialogue around teaching and learning and monitors progress to identify needed adjustments to the school plan as well as opportunities to support the plan. Members of the team include administrators, teachers, support staff, and parents.
- **Student and Staff Support Team:** The SSST promotes desirable social conditions and relationships. It connects all of the school's student services, facilitates the sharing of information and advice, addresses individual student needs, accesses resources outside the school, and develops prevention programs. Membership includes individuals in the school community who possess specialized knowledge, training, or expertise in mental health or child and adolescent development theory and practice.
- **Parent Team:** The PT involves parents in the school by developing activities through which the parents can support the school's social and academic programs. Composed of parents, this team also selects representatives to serve on the School Planning and Management Team.

All three teams operate under three Guiding Principles:

- **No-fault:** No-fault maintains the focus on problem solving rather than placing blame. No-fault does not mean no-accountability. It means *everyone* becomes accountable.
- **Consensus:** Through dialogue and understanding, this decision-making process builds consensus about what is good for children and adolescents. All go with what most think will work—understanding that if it doesn't work, other ideas will be tried.
- **Collaboration:** Collaboration encourages the principal and teams to work together. All agree not to "roadblock" the principal, who has legal responsibility; the principal agrees to be responsive to all members.

Figure 2.2 Schoolhouse model of the Comer Process

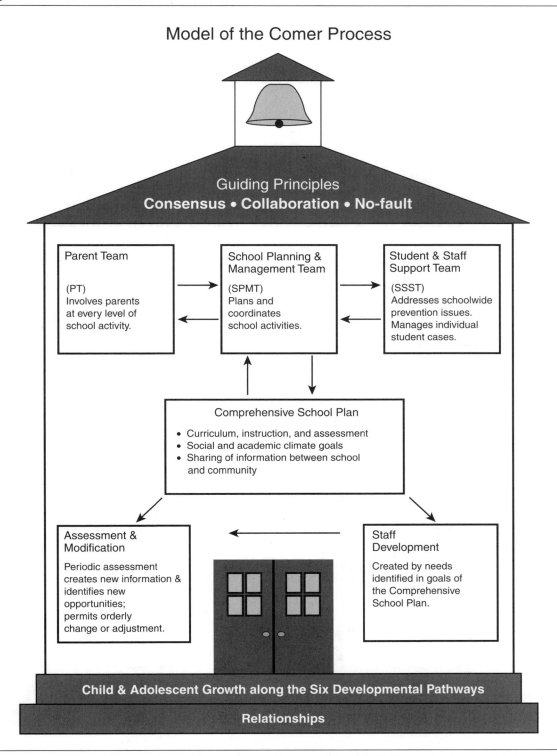

Model of the Comer Process

Guiding Principles
Consensus • Collaboration • No-fault

Parent Team

(PT)
Involves parents
at every level of
school activity.

School Planning &
Management Team

(SPMT)
Plans and
coordinates
school activities.

Student & Staff
Support Team

(SSST)
Addresses schoolwide
prevention issues.
Manages individual
student cases.

Comprehensive School Plan

• Curriculum, instruction, and assessment
• Social and academic climate goals
• Sharing of information between school
 and community

Assessment &
Modification

Periodic assessment
creates new information &
identifies new
opportunities;
permits orderly
change or adjustment.

Staff
Development

Created by needs
identified in goals of
the Comprehensive
School Plan.

Child & Adolescent Growth along the Six Developmental Pathways

Relationships

Figure 2.3 Programa de desarrollo escolar

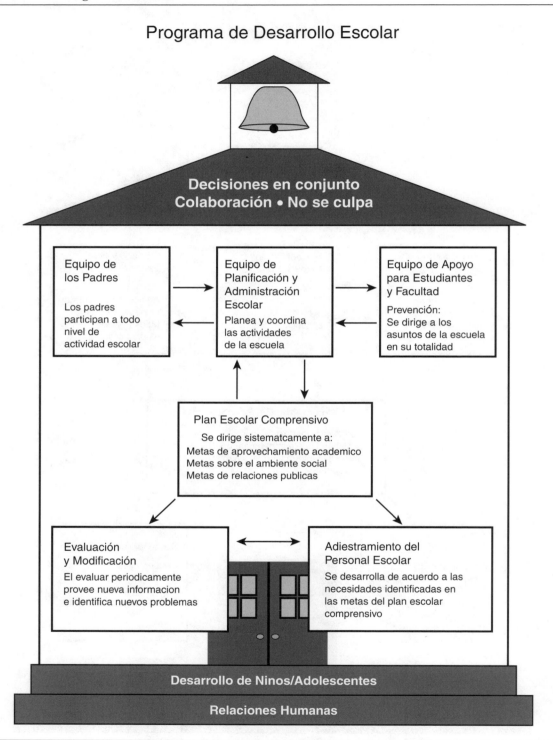

Central to their work are the following three school operations, which are supervised by the School Planning and Management Team:

- **Comprehensive School Plan:** This planning process includes curriculum, instruction, and assessment, as well as social and academic climate goals based on a developmental understanding of students.
- **Staff Development:** Staff development is aligned with the goals of the Comprehensive School Plan; teachers become alert to their own professional development needs and take the lead in designing their own continuing education.
- **Assessment & Modification:** This operation provides new information and identifies new opportunities for support, based on the data of the school's population; data are used to modify the school plan as necessary, thus ensuring that the school is continuously improving its operations.

A school is permitted to call itself "a fully certified SDP school" only after it has completed the full five-year SDP Implementation Life Cycle (see Chapter 18 in *Transforming School Leadership and Management to Support Student Learning and Development*) and the administrators and major teams have met specific behavioral requirements as well as demonstrated excellent knowledge of SDP's approach. Before that time, other labels should be used, for example, "a school in the SDP training program" or "a school in the 1st year (at the 1st stage) of SDP training/implementation."

> For more information on how to become a member of the SDP network, please see our Web site, www.comerprocess.org.

Figure 2.4 School Development Program highlights

- Introduced in 1968 as a process for comprehensive school improvement
- Founded on principles of child development, social relationship theory, and public health
- Nine-element process that fosters positive school climate and creates optimal conditions for teaching and learning
- Not a project or add-on, but a way of managing, organizing, coordinating, and integrating activities
- Provides a strategy for data-driven decision making
- Emphasizes the alignment of curriculum, instruction, and assessment
- Provides schools, districts, and other partners with a framework for communicating and planning to improve conditions for children
- Provides continual support through facilitators and ongoing trainings for adult development as well as child and youth development
- When faithfully and fully implemented, produces extraordinary academic, social, and emotional benefits for the students

THIS FIELD GUIDE

Some members of the school community have a need to approach SDP through a deep understanding of its intellectual foundations. Others need to encounter powerful narratives of how schools improved. Some need to see detailed guidance on what, specifically, they need to do in the classroom. Others need to see how their specialized area fits under SDP's "umbrella." Thus, in our training academies and in this field guide, we provide three types of material:

- narratives that depict SDP in action
- SDP's philosophy
- SDP training materials, including practical exercises

The material in the field guide has been organized in three volumes, as follows:

- *Six Pathways to Healthy Child Development and Academic Success*. The theme of this volume is child and adult development, and the principles that underlie all of our work. To bring out the best in children, we must bring out the best in ourselves.
- *Transforming School Leadership and Management to Support Student Learning and Development*. This volume covers the nine core elements of the Comer Process as they have developed over time.
- *Dynamic Instructional Leadership to Support Student Learning and Development*. This volume continues with Comer Process practices in depth in the classroom, principal leadership, and evaluation of the process. It also describes SDP's approach to systemwide reform that makes the entire district the community of change.

The field guide is a critical resource, but not a replacement for SDP training. Participants in the leadership academies need ways to maintain and review their own experience of the academies once they are back home. They will be responsible for training their school communities in the Comer Process. This field guide will help establish a common language, mind-set, and behavior set within the community.

The take-home message is that *all* members of the school community need to engage in transforming the school—not only the principal or a few key individuals.

RESPONSIBILITIES OF THE SCHOOL COMMUNITY

We believe school communities should

- provide supportive work environments for teachers to maximize their ability to deliver instruction and provide developmental experiences to prepare students for life beyond school
- facilitate positive relationships among parents, students, and school staff to develop the bonds necessary for effective teaching and learning
- be structured to promote collaborative decision making and a culture of inclusion

- promote learning as a lifelong process
- value cultural, linguistic, and ethnic differences to enhance the educational process for all people
- use data from all levels of the system—student, school, and the district—to inform educational policies and practices
- view change as an ongoing process guided by continuous constructive feedback
- design curriculum, instruction, and assessment to align with national, state, and local standards and promote child and community development
- provide administrators with the support they need to lead and manage schools
- promote organizational coherence among school boards, educators, and parents
- provide a sound education with an emphasis on civic responsibility

An education system that fosters child and adolescent development will make it possible to maintain and improve our democratic society.

3

Schools in Society

Carmen S. Gonzalez

Schools are microcosms of their neighborhoods, and when neighborhoods are in crisis, schools suffer. SDP moves schools out of a crisis mode, and helps to heal communities through well-organized teams that respond quickly to the needs of students and their families. In one impoverished Brooklyn, New York, community, the elementary school's Child Study Team has been delivering much-needed social, health, and psychological services. The positive outcomes of this attention and the related change in student and staff beliefs about achieving success have helped to transform a failing institution into one of the fastest-improving schools in New York City.

A TOUGH BROOKLYN NEIGHBORHOOD

Our school is a prekindergarten through sixth-grade elementary school with 600 children. We're located in a tough Brooklyn neighborhood: The poverty rate of our school population is 94 percent. In the 2000–2001 school year, 56 children had asthma, 13 of whom were in the American Lung Association's Open Airways program.[1] Three children were medicated for ADHD. Five children had anemia or were anemic—in some cases caused by sickle cell disease and in others caused by malnutrition. In one case that was very serious the child had to be rushed to the hospital. He had come from a refugee camp in Guyana. Sitting in the back of the classroom, he had passed out. The teacher sent down the emergency pass, so I knew that as the principal I had to get upstairs immediately. I ran. The child wouldn't wake up. We called for the nurse. She came up. We called 911. They came. The child's sickle cell anemia was so bad that he needed a transfusion. He had no doctor. He had no health plan. We were able to help him immediately. We also helped him in an ongoing way before anything else really serious happened to him.

Other health incidents have happened in our school over the past five years: One child had high blood pressure, six children with cardiac conditions were under parental supervision, three children had digestive disorders, two children had juvenile arthritis, seven had lead poisonings, 10 had nosebleeds, 12 children were obese, two children had physical impairments, four children suffered renal disorder, one child had a seizure, and 176 children had vision impairments. We have conducted 166 hearing screenings. We had two children with skin disorders, 10 cases of lice, and 18 cases of ringworm. We had two cases of chicken pox, one case of rheumatic fever, one diabetic child, one child with a very serious muscle disorder, and two children with scoliosis. As of late fall 2002, one child was in a coma. That case was very serious. The child is now in a children's hospital receiving chemotherapy for his blood condition. He bruises at the touch. (Imagine if you were the teacher of this child and you weren't informed of his condition!)

> There are 600 children in the school. Our Child Study Team handled 1,428 cases this past year.

How do I know all this? These cases were discussed in our Child Study Team, which is more popularly known throughout the School Development Program (SDP) as the Student and Staff Support Team (SSST). The SSST is an integral part of the structure of SDP—it's not a separate entity, but rather a contributing factor to everything that happens in the school. Our Child Study Team handled 1,428 cases in the 2000–2001 school year (some students were seen multiple times).

OUR CHILD STUDY TEAM HAS A SYSTEMATIC PROCESS

All the teachers, parents, and kids know the way in which the Child Study Team operates. If the teachers have concerns, they can make referrals in writing, they can tell us verbally, or they can just call us on the phone and say they have a crisis in the classroom and can we intervene? And the parents, through the parent newsletter and the calendar, know that team meetings are scheduled every Monday morning from 9:00 a.m. to 11:00 a.m. They are welcome to walk in.

As the cases come in we prioritize them and discuss each one separately. We do interventions or present classroom lessons for teachers who have consistent issues with children or classroom management, or with very sensitive topics, such as the September 11, 2001, crisis when the World Trade Center and the Pentagon were attacked. Basically, this system works to make the school community understand that there are people in the school who care about kids, the parents, and staff. The parents are our largest clientele. The children also know they can tell us if they're having problems with a particular adult, or if someone has been disrespectful to them, or if they are just very depressed and need to talk.

Thirty-six percent of our students are foster children (i.e., living under the care of someone other than a parent or both parents). Through them, we are connected strongly to community organizations, as several of their social workers are based in the school two or more days a week in order to serve the children and their adult caregivers. The social workers are also part of the team. (Originally we receive grants to support these services, but the results were so positive that now the school district operates similar programs in five schools.)

It is our school policy that no child is referred to special education or to any kind of program outside the school without having gone through the process of review from the Child Study Team. It is the backbone of our school.

BEING ON A TEAM HELPS US TO COPE

Some cases are very difficult. In one instance, a parent came in because she wanted help with her child. She started by presenting an extremely negative picture of her second grader: The child doesn't do this, doesn't do that, doesn't listen to me. We sent for the child. The child came and sat next to his parent. He crossed his arms and just looked down. He wouldn't look up. We tried to talk to him. He wouldn't talk.

Finally, I said, "Well, we can't help you if you don't let us in and let us understand your problems."

He looked at his mother and said, "She hates me." It was as simple as that.

At that point, the social worker turned around and said to the mother, "We need to talk, and we need to talk at length, because your child is feeling very strongly about how you are interacting with him."

The parent turned around and was ready to slap the living daylights out of the child. We stopped her from doing that. We asked her to please step out of the room. We asked the child his version of what was going on.

The little boy just sat there and cried. He told us: Mom uses him and abuses him. If he doesn't cook her food right, she kicks him. If he doesn't iron right, she belts him. His story went on and on.

The psychologist asked him, "If there's one thing that we can get your mother to do, what would that be?"

He said, "I just want her to hug me once." We all broke down in tears. It was so hard to stop the emotion.

We brought the mother back in. We told her: "Your child needs an expression of love. Just for once, would you hug your child?" Do you know that she would not hug her child? She would not. I'm sharing this with you so you understand that some cases are very difficult.

We're still working with the mother and son. We told the boy that when he's good in school, we'd call his mother to tell her the good things instead of the bad things. We also gave the mother an ultimatum about the alleged physical abuse, and it stopped.

INTERVENTIONS THAT WORK

We're no longer operating in a crisis mode. Because the Child Study Team is well trained and has trained the school community, everyone can say, "I know what I'm doing, and I can do it well." Teachers routinely intervene with parents who may be upset and acting out. Prior to the team structure, no one would take ownership. Everyone would watch a crisis, comment about it, and not do anything about it. It's completely different now. Everyone is a stakeholder here.

Because of this commitment and involvement, we've come up with several successful interventions that have really worked.

The Alarm Clock Program

When I first came to the school, my children were coming in at 10:00 a.m., thinking that this was not a problem. "You're lucky I'm here, girl." That's what they told me: "You're lucky I'm here. You're lucky I woke up!" The daily attendance rate was 74 percent at that time. We worked on it, and it inched up, but we could never get 90 percent.

We analyzed the late logs and the absence logs. When I complete the log sheets, I don't write just the child's name, I also write the reason for the tardiness. We found that a lot of students get themselves up. They dress themselves. They make their own breakfast. I had one child burned all the way down his body because hot oatmeal spilled on him. These students are on their own.

We thought and thought about it. Finally, my attendance coordinator said, "These students need their own alarm clocks." We went to the businesses in the area and asked if they could support the children and the program. We raised about $500 and we bought 100 alarm clocks. If children are chronically late or chronically absent, we don't give them late detention. We give them early detention. They have to show up at 8:00 a.m. for a week. The attendance coordinator meets with them. We feed them. They get their breakfast and then homework support. The attendance coordinator teaches them how to set the clock. They use the clock in the morning to monitor their time. They keep journals. How long does it take you to get dressed? How long does it take you to eat? How long does it take you to walk from home to school? If we change their wake-up time, we change their internal clocks. We can't change everything, but we can change that internal clock. We got them up earlier and to school on time. (In fact, at least one parent has used her son's clock in order to make sure she got to a job interview on time.) Guess what my attendance rate was that year: 91 percent. The superintendent gave me a plaque. I was so happy. As of November 2002, it was 94 percent!

> When I first came to the school, my children were coming in at 10:00 a.m., thinking that this was not a problem. "You're lucky I'm here, girl." That's what they told me. The daily attendance rate was 74 percent at that time. As of November 2002, it was 94 percent!

Support for Social and Emotional Development

Joey (pseudonym) came to us from another country at the beginning of the 2000–2001 school year. We conducted a case conference about him on September 17. He had received special education services all his life. This was the first time he came to a system where he was integrated with his own age group. In his country, special education students are placed according to their cognitive level. He was 12 years old and had been placed with kindergartners, so Joey had no concept of how to interact with his peers.

We requested a complete medical and psychological evaluation for him. During the case study we identified an additional problem that was previously unknown. Joey confused everything that he took in visually. The psychologist told us that it was a rare form of disability. His visual processing did not conform to reality. Because he was 11, going on 12, we had placed him in the fifth grade. The teacher from the fifth grade was upset: "What am I going to do with Joey? He can't read! Ms. Gonzalez, please!" We then placed him with a fourth-grade teacher who was very nurturing and caring. We all worked continuously with him. We also hoped that by the end of the school year Joey would learn to socialize with others his own age. The first time Joey smiled was when his team won the baseball competition. The class held him up on their shoulders and rah-rah-ed him. We knew that we had made at least one break-through with Joey, and that was in his social skills. He's in our fifth-grade special edu-cation class, and he is receiving additional services (occupational therapy, physical therapy, and psychological services). He's reading on a second-grade level, comes to school every day, and smiles all the time.

Ongoing Support After Crisis Intervention

Benny's (pseudonym) dad was in an insulin coma for six months. One day his mother came running into school and said, "My husband is in the hospital, and I don't know what happened!" We were very concerned about Benny because he was very close to his dad. He wouldn't talk with anybody. He wasn't doing any work. He was just sitting in class with his head down, and that was it. He wouldn't cry, he wouldn't whimper, he wouldn't do anything. We evaluated him in the Child Study Team and found out that he was a diabetic, too. Now the school nurse supervises Benny. Miraculously, the father began to recover. Benny's doing very well in school, and he has made friends.

The In-House Suspension Program and Acts of Kindness

How else does the Child Study Team receive cases? Behavioral problems are a large source of referral. With an in-house suspension program piloted by the team, 54 suspensions in the 1999–2000 school year were reduced to just one suspension in the 2000–2001 school year. The program is supported by its own discrete space, a social worker, a counselor, and teachers. Students do all their classwork, which is then graded. They write a great deal reflecting on themselves and on what they could have done differently to avoid suspension. They are not allowed to socialize or play or eat with their friends. We make it harsh because we don't want them to like it. We want them not to want to go back to the suspension room. They learn very quickly that it's easier to do an Act of Kindness than it is to do in-house suspension.

What is an Act of Kindness? I believe that it's not enough to say, "I'm sorry." For instance, a girl is about to sit down, a boy pulls the chair out from under her, and she falls on the ground. She's hurt—but more than this, she's embarrassed. He can't just say, "I'm sorry." Yes, he's sorry but he's going to do it again because the only conse-quence he had was saying, "I'm sorry." We handle this situation by instituting Acts of Kindness. For two weeks, the child who pulled out the girl's chair must pull out the chair for her to sit on. In the cafeteria, he must bring her lunch to her table. When she's finished he must remove her tray. He must carry her book bag throughout the school and hold the doors open for her. After three days that boy is pleading, "Please, please—enough, enough!" I say, "Not until the girl—who got her feelings hurt more than anything else—not until she says it's okay will it be okay." Usually the victimized child comes to me and says, "We're friends now." Only then do I accept the apology. I make them go through Acts of Kindness because I feel that they have civil and ethical responsibilities.

My school is spotless. If there's graffiti in the bathroom, I find out who did it. Not only do they go to in-house suspension, but they also spend a week with the custodian. They don't wear their uniform? They must collect uniforms for needy children. For other infractions, they have to read to younger children for 10 hours. It works. I have very few children in in-house suspension. The ones in Acts of Kindness eventually come to me and say, "Ms. Gonzalez, you were right. That wasn't very nice, what I did." So they stop that kind of behavior.

ACTION-ORIENTED SELF-ASSESSMENT

The Child Study Team assesses itself three times a year. We see how we are doing because we want to get our bearings. Are we on the right track? What, specifically, are we doing? We ask ourselves these questions: Are we communicating our vision that all children can succeed? Do we encourage teachers to assess students' learning styles? Do we constantly practice and apply the Comer principles? Do we fully and fairly participate in all child study conferences? Do we seek volunteers and tutors? Do we seek grants? Do we take care that our community partnerships are healthy? A good Child Study Team is your right arm. If you're meeting the needs of all the children, there aren't going to be many serious problems in your school. If you provide the social and emotional care and the psychological and physical care—if you get glasses for the kids and a serious reading program, and they're happy in school because they play an instrument or they're running on the track team—then you're not going to have problems with test scores. The students will be healthy and accomplishing all around.

WE ARE ON THE RIGHT TRACK

The same day on which this chapter was completed the school district released the 2001–2002 summary of school performance. It showed how well the students performed on the Math and English Language Arts (ELA) standardized tests. Schools in the district were ranked based on the percentage of students who had moved from the lower levels of achievement to the highest level. *P.S. 46 was ranked number one.*

NOTE

1. The Open Airways program trains teachers, parents, and students to manage asthma and asthma medications, and to respond appropriately to respiratory emergencies.

READ MORE ABOUT . . .

For information on the Student and Staff Support Team, see "The Student and Staff Support Team and the Coordination of Student Services," Chapter 11 in *Transforming School Leadership and Management to Support Student Learning and Development: The Field Guide to Comer Schools in Action* in this series.

4

Child Development Is the Foundation of Education

Fay E. Brown and Joanne N. Corbin

The School Development Program (SDP) is based on the holistic premise of six pathways as a foundation for successful learning and healthy development. This framework helps educators and parents to understand their students and themselves better, and encourages everyone in the school to create a healthier climate while working toward greater academic success. The highly successful training activities presented here will help schools use the pathways framework to address student, adult, and community issues.

MEETING THE NEEDS OF EVERY CHILD

Schools currently operate in an "accountability era" in which the major focus appears to be the improvement of test scores. Within the context of this myopic focus, the student often gets lost. While it is important to increase test scores, there also needs to be a focus on two far more important objectives: developing a comprehensive understanding of what needs to be done in the best interests of every child, and then making the deliberate effort to meet the needs of every child effectively.

In this chapter, we reinforce an argument that has been articulated for many years by James P. Comer, M.D. That is, we must focus our attention on every child in a holistic manner if we are going to plan effectively to meet that child's needs. If the goal of parents and educators is to help all children develop to become the best that they are capable of becoming, then knowledge of how children grow, develop, and learn is pivotal to the plan of ensuring that they do become their best. To that end, in this chapter we provide specific information about the six developmental pathways (physical, cognitive, psychological, language, social, and ethical) that form the foundation of the SDP model. We also provide recommendations and examples of how to use the developmental pathways framework as a tool for ensuring the holistic development of children and adolescents.

THE SIX DEVELOPMENTAL PATHWAYS

In most schools and classrooms the curriculum is driven by the need to make students proficient in their intellectual or cognitive skills. In addition, based on the belief that language mediates cognitive development, the improvement of students' language skills is a priority. Unfortunately, there has not been enough of an effort to assist students in their development in other areas. More specifically, attention must be given to students to ensure their development along each of the six critical pathways.

Physical Pathway

Promoting children's and adolescents' development along the physical pathway means providing opportunities that help them increase their capacity for the healthy functioning of all the systems in the body. This encompasses physical health, nutrition, and responsible decision making, particularly regarding adolescent sexual conduct and use of drugs and alcohol.

Teachers and other school staff need to find creative and meaningful ways to support the physical needs of students, particularly those in schools that are eliminating recess and extracurricular activities. The opportunity to release pent-up energy in structured and supervised ways can decrease physical acting out behaviors and help students return to their classroom work with more focus.

Cognitive Pathway

Promoting children's and adolescents' development along the cognitive pathway means helping them increase their capacity to think for themselves, to plan strategically and effectively, to solve problems in different contexts, to set goals for themselves, and to work with focused attention to accomplish those goals. Development along this pathway also includes the ability to recognize when one's own resources are not sufficient to carry out a task and when to ask for and receive help.

An effective teacher has an understanding of how children learn, and employs techniques that can enhance children's ability to gain specific academic knowledge. For example, we encountered a fifth-grade teacher who determined at the beginning of the school year that most of the students in the class did not know their multiplication tables. Although the curriculum for the year started with the multiplication of fractions, this teacher knew that without having achieved the prerequisite cognitive task of understanding basic multiplication, it would be impossible for students to understand the concept of multiplication of fractions. The teacher began with teaching the multiplication tables, and three months later had built a foundation on which to teach the multiplication of fractions. By contrast, the teacher's colleagues, who had merely followed the curriculum, found that their students who had not mastered basic multiplication experienced significant conceptualization difficulties.

Psychological Pathway

Promoting children's and adolescents' development along the psychological pathway means helping them increase their capacity for self-acceptance and self-confidence during the ongoing process of identity formation. This includes feelings of adequacy, efficacy, and competence. When a student feels competent in completing a task or solving a problem, this feeling may propel that student into an action often expressed as strong academic performance. Conversely, if a student feels a lack of competence or has feelings of inferiority (Erikson, 1963, p. 188), these feelings can serve as demotivating forces on the learning process, and can result in weak academic performance. A focus on the psychological pathway also includes training children and adolescents to manage their emotions in socially accepted ways. Children and adolescents have to be taught that, along life's path, everyone gets angry at some point but that feeling angry is not the problem; rather, it is one's actions that may become problematic. Therefore children and adolescents need to be taught coping mechanisms and problem-solving skills.

Sometimes, what makes students lose confidence or become upset is not apparent to others around the student, including the adults. The establishment of a safe classroom climate is essential for fostering a well-developed sense of confidence. Some classes have rules that students may not laugh at or tease one another. Some classes have safe areas or time-out areas; students who need a few minutes to regroup can go there and then reenter the activity without bringing attention to themselves. It is only in safe classrooms that students feel that they can take risks as they learn.

Language Pathway

Promoting children's and adolescents' development along the language pathway means helping them increase their capacity for receptive and expressive language in a variety of contexts. For students to become successful and productive in our diverse society, there is an increasing need for both oral and written language fluency.

Language is a part of everything that occurs within the school. This includes the tone of the spoken word, phrasing that appears on signs in the classrooms or halls, public address system announcements, rules about talking or not talking in the cafeteria, and greetings at the beginning of the school day. The congruency of the primary language of the school and the languages of the homes from which students come, and the level of vocabulary used with students impact their linguistic progress. To ensure students' mastery of language, teachers must not assume that all students have the same background regarding language exposure or experience; they must deliberately teach and model language and communication skills appropriate for the school environment, and enhancing to the overall development of the language pathway.

Social Pathway

Promoting children's and adolescents' development along the social pathway means providing opportunities that help them increase their capacity to build healthy relationships across the range of human diversity. This includes the ability to interact with those who may be different from themselves, and the ability to demonstrate empathy toward others. Adults need to model the appropriate social behaviors that they wish to see in children.

Social interactions within schools send important messages about how to treat individuals. When staff members walk by one another without acknowledgment, a powerful message is sent to the students about how to behave toward others. Appropriate and positive messages among the school constituents are exhibited by audience behavior during assemblies. These social interchanges indicate whether or not there is an appropriate climate of respect, emotional safety, and sense of inclusion or exclusion. Climate permeates the whole school.

One school within the SDP network began to develop classroom as well as schoolwide codes of behavior. Initially, this effort addressed such physical behavior as fighting. In subsequent years it expanded to include verbal conflicts such as name-calling and malicious teasing. This is only one of many examples of the overlap among the developmental pathways; in this instance both the language pathway and the social pathway were addressed.

Ethical Pathway

Promoting children's and adolescents' development along the ethical pathway means providing opportunities to help them increase their capacity for behaving with justice and fairness toward themselves and others. This includes helping them to understand the importance of the integrity and respect for self and others. As with the other pathways, students—especially young students—benefit from having appropriate adult role models.

Encouraging students to participate in designing the classroom codes for verbal and nonverbal behavior allows them to apply the ethical pathway to their everyday lives. Some students who have not had experience with this type of responsibility may require more guidance from adults. Students who are involved in the creation of these guiding principles for the classroom experience a greater sense of ownership and responsibility for their behavior, as well as responsibility for the well-being of their classmates. This practice mirrors the use of the guiding principles (no-fault, consensus, and collaboration) by adults on the SDP teams.

RATIONALE FOR THE PATHWAYS FRAMEWORK

Children will naturally grow and develop unless biological or environmental factors impede their growth. The quality of development can be undermined if the adults around these children are not deliberate and intentional in their efforts to support it. The pathways framework organizes and governs that support in a meaningful and effective way that will ensure positive outcomes for students.

A development perspective

- maintains the focus of the adults on children
- extends the principle of no-fault problem solving to the relationships with children
- provides a framework for adults to consider children's behavior in a larger context, offering the "big picture" of each child versus a myopic judgment
- enables adults to develop and implement strategies that promote the health and positive self-esteem of students—individually and collectively

USING THE PATHWAYS FRAMEWORK TO ADDRESS STUDENT ISSUES

As members of the SDP national staff, we work in schools throughout the country. Walking through a school can tell us a lot about the school's climate, academic focus, openness to the community, and attitude toward the students and adults within the school. We see some students change classes in an orderly and directed manner; elsewhere we see students run and crash into lockers or push their way down flights of stairs. We see classrooms where students sleep on desks during a class, and those in which students engage with the teacher about a particular topic. We have students or teachers come up to us and ask whether we are the new teacher or a substitute teacher. Those in a different school ask if they can help us or if they can show us to the main office. We hear teachers and administrators yell at students in ways that would be classified as verbal assault or abuse. We experience other teachers and administrators finding a quiet place to talk with a student who has violated a code of conduct. Some hallways are clean, while a walk-through in others exposes trash. These snapshots of some everyday school experiences serve as examples of how a school's focus can have a strong impact on student and staff morale, on teachers' and students' expectations, and on the broader learning environment.

Training Activity 4.1: Using the pathways to identify student issues and behaviors at your school

At a recent SDP 102 Leadership Academy, we asked training groups to engage in an activity. This activity may be completed by everyone, including school administrators, teachers, parents, administrative assistants, custodial staff, cafeteria staff, security staff, library media specialists, school nurse, school social worker, school psychologist, and student council. The activity begins with the following questions:

1. Given your various roles, what are the issues/behaviors within your classroom and school context that impact student achievement and overall development?

The following is an example of a combined response from various groups:

> Attendance (student and staff), tardiness, mobility rate, poverty, neighborhood crime (prostitution, gangs, violence), medical issues such as diabetes and asthma, abuse/neglect, incarceration of family members, uneducated parents, overcrowded classrooms, homelessness (no access to phone), foster homes, language barrier, lack of T.L.C., lack of appropriate social services, transience, drugs, inadequate resources, lack of parental involvement, lack of trust, conflict among students, low expectations, poor teacher-student relationships, teacher burnout, and teacher shortage.

2. How would you respond to that question in your school? You may respond as an individual, as a grade-level team member, as a member of the School Planning and Management Team, as a member of the Student and Staff Support Team, or in whatever capacity you work in your school.

   Based on the reasons we articulated for the use of a developmental perspective, this activity is intended to help adults think about and talk about students' behavior and issues in a decidedly descriptive manner. That is, it is intended (1) to help adults examine students' issues and behaviors in a no-fault way, and (2) to encourage them to consider how those issues and behaviors may impact students' learning and development.

There are two other parts to this activity:

3. Use the pathways framework to categorize those issues and behaviors.

4. Keeping in mind the strengths and weaknesses of your classroom, school, and district, what are the most practical solutions for addressing those behaviors to ensure students' learning and development?

By requesting schools to categorize students' issues and behaviors within the pathways framework, we encourage the use of the pathways as an evaluative tool. When students exhibit certain behaviors or present certain issues that adults consider to be inappropriate or detrimental to their learning and development, their nonverbal communication is meaningful. There are reasons why students behave in particular ways. For example, students may sleep in classes because of something physical, cognitive, or psychological. From a physical perspective, it could be a symptom of insufficient rest at night or dehydration. From a cognitive perspective, it could be the result of boredom with the particular task. Psychologically, sleeping could be a defense mechanism that students use to disguise their feelings of inadequacy if they are not performing on a par with their classmates or consider themselves to be inferior to those classmates. They may also crave some attention from the teacher and realize that falling asleep will bring them the attention they seek.

Categorizing those behaviors within the pathways framework forces us to think of a number of possibilities for students' presenting issues. This strategy prevents the adults from jumping to conclusions too quickly, and sometimes, erroneously. In other words, by examining those behaviors through a developmental lens, the adults get a more accurate picture of children. They are then better equipped to implement developmentally appropriate and relevant measures to address those behaviors.

Once the particular behaviors have been categorized within the pathways framework, teams find it more manageable to consider strategies that when applied, will be in the best interests of children. The message is not that the pathways are separate and should be handled as such. Quite the contrary: The pathways are all interconnected and interrelated. By paying attention to each one when evaluating student behavior, we increase the possibility that the adults will consider the needs of the "whole child," and we maximize the student's chances of receiving comprehensive and appropriate services.

Additional Examples of Using the Pathways Framework

For many teachers, keeping up with the everyday challenges and expectations in the classroom and the school environment is sufficient and, at times, overwhelming. Initially, teachers are presented with the notion of using the pathways framework to guide student planning, instruction, evaluation, and their interaction with students. Teachers typically respond, "This is too much," or, "We don't have enough time in a school day to take on any additional responsibilities." The pathways framework is not intended to make teachers do more work. It is to advocate that some of them work differently. Once they realize that in some ways they have been using the framework unintentionally and intuitively, they find that it becomes a beneficial tool and provides an enjoyable manner in which to work. One way to start is by categorizing everything that you are currently doing according to the pathways. At the school level, this categorization will help teachers create a common language among themselves, a common language with students, and also a common language with parents.

Training Activity 4.2: Using the pathways for curriculum, instruction, and classroom management

As a team, brainstorm strategies that may be implemented to demonstrate the use of the pathways framework in instruction and other classroom practices. Consider the following sample of responses from participants at our different academies:

Physical

- Properly maintain the building to ensure a safe environment.
- Partner with health care agency in the community.
- Vary seating arrangements in the classroom.
- Allow frequent opportunities for movement.
- Allow in-class "snack time" and encourage healthy eating habits.
- Provide water breaks.
- Be flexible regarding bathroom breaks.
- Use class meetings to teach responsible decision making regarding smoking, alcohol and drug use, and sexual behaviors.

- Invite the school nurse into the classroom to discuss issues regarding dental and personal hygiene, and to screen for sight, hearing, and speech problems.
- Provide training for parents regarding proper nutrition.
- Institute programs such as "Coats for Kids," especially for homeless students.

Cognitive

- Use hands-on tools that give children the resources to solve problems and figure out answers for themselves.
- Facilitate brainstorming sessions to spark ideas and establish cooperative groups to promote the exchange of ideas.
- Encourage journal writing/creative writing.
- Encourage appropriate Internet searches.
- Assign book reports/research projects.
- Encourage students' use of their imagination, especially in writing narratives.
- Give students the opportunity for self-monitoring and self–peer evaluation.
- Use open-ended student-created rubrics.
- Use open-ended/inquiry-type questions to examine cause/effect, predictions, synthesis, application, analysis, and evaluation.
- Use manipulatives.

Psychological

- Provide conflict resolution/peer mediation.
- Designate a "cool off" chair.
- Encourage journaling to express feelings.
- Conduct class meetings to establish an environment in which students feel safe to express their feelings.
- Institute sharing circles.
- Design a reward/reinforcement system to promote academic achievement and positive behaviors.
- Accommodate individual student "special time" with the teacher.
- Know students' names and personal information about them.
- Clarify classroom responsibilities that establish every student as an important stakeholder in the classroom.
- Give students roles to play that allow them to feel a sense of ownership, belonging, and pride.
- Recognize the special gifts and talents in every child.

Language

- Use comfortable topics (comfort zone) to encourage students to express themselves.
- Introduce Readers' Theater, that is, do familiar plays or stories and allow students to present them the way they want to.
- Conduct small group meetings.
- Expose students to different genres.
- Encourage shared stories.

- Require oral presentations.
- Apply appropriate critique procedures.
- Encourage role playing.
- Conduct listening skill activities.
- Institute Drop Everything and Read (DEAR).
- Create a situation with an intended goal, for example
  library situation—establish a conducive conversational tone such as whispering
  mock job interviews—discuss strengths and weaknesses at the end
  mock trial—debate different points of view
  speeches—teach effective public speaking skills such as appropriate eye contact, articulation, poise, and delivery
  videotape students giving speeches—allow students to view themselves and each other and offer constructive feedback

Social

- Conduct gender-based meetings.
- Encourage role playing/drama productions.
- Implement a buddy system: lower grades teaming with upper grades.
- Organize a pen pals project.
- Institute a community project, for example, a leaf-collection project for the elderly.
- Conduct relationship-building activities to establish trust and respect.
- Arrange classroom seating in circle format: each voice heard, all faces seen.
- Introduce a multicultural day.
- Build cultural relevance into lesson plans.
- Utilize conflict resolution/peer mediation.
- Encourage cooperative learning.
- Institute cooperative games, for example, "center time" to teach sharing and cooperation.
- Provide character education with monthly theme.
- Identify classroom managers or helpers.
- Encourage participation in student organizations and clubs.

Ethical

- Help students to understand consensus decision making and no-fault problem solving.
- Role-play proper behavior.
- Involve students in the process of developing classroom rules and consequences.
- Institute diversity grouping.
- Allow student expression without fear of ridicule.
- Create a multicultural curriculum.
- Provide character education.
- Use the curriculum to bring to the students' attention examples of right and wrong behavior or choices.
- Use literature for examples of good versus evil.

- Teach respect and understanding through discussions of differences among people.
- Encourage students to consider the perspective of others.
- Talk about your own experiences.
- Be a role model.

What were your insights as you completed this activity? Did you find that you and your colleagues have been implementing strategies that promote students' development along each of the six pathways? Like some of the responses shared above, did you find that many of your activities can be categorized under more than one pathway? If you answered in the affirmative to the latter question, you have just substantiated the fact that the pathways are not separate and discreet, but are interdependent and interrelated.

WRITING LESSON PLANS USING THE PATHWAYS FRAMEWORK

Teachers have found it beneficial to write their lesson plans using the framework of the pathways. They have found that this strategy highlights strengths and weaknesses in their lessons. For example, a majority of the activities in their lesson plans provide support for students' learning and development along the cognitive and language pathways. Because their students sometimes work in groups, they may be providing support for the social pathway. They often find that there is a need to build in more activities to provide support for students' learning and development along the physical, ethical, and psychological pathways.

Training Activity 4.3: Aligning your lesson plans with the pathways

How does your own plan measure up in terms of the pathways framework? Using your own lesson plan and the pathways worksheet (Figure 4.1), please complete the following task:

1. Identify the pathways that are evident in your lesson plan.

2. Are you satisfied with your findings?

3. If there is evidence that certain pathways are not being supported or promoted through the execution of your plan, modify your plan to reflect most or all of the pathways. You may consider completing this task with members of your grade-level team. If you write weekly lesson plans, you may find that all six pathways may not be given attention every day and every week. If, however, you see a pattern in which over an entire month you are not able to identify specific strategies or activities aimed at promoting certain pathways (e.g., the ethical or psychological), then modify your plan to incorporate activities to support those pathways. Remember that the aim is to enhance student development along all six pathways.

Figure 4.1 Worksheet for aligning lesson plans with the six developmental pathways

Lesson Plan: Content Area/ Strategies/ Activities	Developmental Pathway				
	Physical	Cognitive	Psychological	Language	Social	Ethical

USING THE PATHWAYS FRAMEWORK TO ADDRESS ADULT ISSUES

The pathways framework is not intended for use only with children. It has also proven to be an excellent tool to help adults evaluate and plan for the self and others. Consider completing the following activity.

Training Activity 4.4: Using the pathways to assess your own well-being and interactions with students

Keeping in mind that a healthy adult is more capable of helping to develop healthy children, use the pathways framework to examine yourself in the following manner:

1. Reflect on yourself within the past month.

2. Rate your well-being along the six pathways.

3. What were some of the factors that contributed positively to your state of being?

4. What, if any, were some of the negative contributing factors?

5. What impact did your state of being (negative or positive) have on your interaction with others—particularly children?

6. Using the pathways framework, design a monthly plan for yourself that ensures or at least promotes optimal health along each of the six pathways.

At first, you may not feel comfortable about completing this activity. It is often easier to deal with external issues rather than those that are internal and personal. Furthermore, as educators we tend to be so busy teaching and taking care of everything and everyone else, that it becomes difficult to take time for self-reflection and planning to ensure our own holistic health. Thus we encourage you to take the time to complete this activity.

This activity is designed to help us become more cognizant of ourselves. The activity helps us become more intentional and deliberate about planning strategies to promote and ensure our well-being in a holistic manner. If, as adults, we are more in tune with ourselves, more aware of the changes that we undergo daily, more aware of the things that make us happy and those that make us sad, then there is a greater possibility that we will be kinder to ourselves and to others—particularly the children with whom we interact every day. Berk (1991) reminds us that our behavior is not simply a response to the actions of others, but that it is also a manifestation of our inner psychological states (p. 265). The more in tune we are with ourselves, the more likely it will be that we will engage appropriate coping strategies. And, in turn, the less likely it will be that we will offend others or impede the learning and development of our students.

USING THE PATHWAYS FRAMEWORK TO CREATE A CULTURE FOR THE SCHOOL COMMUNITY

At this point, it seems pertinent to reiterate that we are operating in a test-driven society in which the emphasis is on raising the test scores for individual students, thus increasing the academic status and ranking of individual schools. The concept of holistic development of students may seem foreign to individual and collective policy writers. To advocate educating children from a developmental perspective seems, literally, to be going against the grain of the expected, the accepted, and the norm. Therefore, if schools expect to make an important and lasting contribution to the lives of the students placed in their care, they have to make a concerted effort to permeate the entire school community with developmental knowledge and the use of a developmental framework.

The School Planning and Management Team

A pivotal place to start this effort is with the School Planning and Management Team (SPMT). The SPMT is the central decision-making body in the school (see McLaughlin, Ennis, & Hernández, 2004). It is the body that writes and monitors the Comprehensive School Plan (Maholmes, 2004) and sanctions the different programs that are implemented throughout the school.

The programs that are implemented in our schools have a decided impact on the culture of the school. To permeate the school's culture with a developmental understanding—and, in particular, with the use of the pathways framework—we should make a concerted effort to use this framework as a barometer to assess the relevance of our programs. The following question is at the heart of making program implementation decisions: Are these programs student focused, and, as such, will they be in the best interests of our students?

Assess each program that you are implementing or are planning to implement: Examine the program by creating a grid that helps you look at the populations being served and the pathways being addressed. In particular, if a program is truly going to meet the needs of students, it should address the students' development along most, if not all, of the six pathways. Some programs tend to address the cognitive, language, and perhaps the social, without much attention to the physical, ethical, and psychological. Figure 4.2 will help you identify the strengths and gaps in your current programs in terms of their potential to support students' development along all six pathways. If using this chart helps you to recognize gaps, then implement a plan to modify that program. Sometimes only slight modifications are needed to accomplish this task.

The Student and Staff Support Team

Decisions made by the Student and Staff Support Team (SSST) about individual students or groups of students can impede or promote students' learning and development. Generally, when a student has been referred to the SSST, it is because the student is perceived to need help to deal with "inappropriate, acting out behaviors" or to sort out other behaviors that have been deemed challenging or problematic to

Figure 4.2 Student-focused planning form

Program	Populations Served			Developmental Pathways Addressed					
	Grade	Gender	Special Characteristics	Physical	Cognitive	Psychological	Language	Social	Ethical

a teacher, a parent, or other adult. It is critical for the SSST to have all the relevant information about that student at the time of referral so that it can make a decision in the best interests of the child. The pathways framework proves very beneficial in gathering relevant information and in making a meaningful and fair decision. Several years ago, the members of the Prince George's County Comer Network developed a form that has proven invaluable to members of many SSSTs. With the permission of that office, the form appears here as Figure 4.3. SSSTs that do not have a similar tool may use this form when making decisions.

The top section of the form requires some specific information about the individual student (e.g., date of birth, attendance history, and health condition). The bottom portion requires information from the referring individual about the student within the framework of the six pathways. This form makes a powerful contribution to the creation and promotion of a developmentally oriented culture in the school community. It enables the referring individual to look at the student through a developmental lens. That individual must provide information about the student in terms of the student's strengths and needs along each of the relevant pathways. In addition, the referring individual must describe any interventions that have been tried with the student in terms of the pathways. Discussion notes are expected to be made within the parameters of the pathways. Through the integration of the referral and the pathways framework, the members of the SSST "meet" that student from a developmental perspective. SSST members evaluate the student using a developmental lens, and make decisions about that student that are developmentally appropriate as a result of that focus.

The SSST is so named because it is expected to provide support to the staff as well as to the students. The team helps different staff members become aware of and use the pathways framework in their various interactions with students. Creating a school culture that promotes students' learning and development requires all staff members to become cognizant of the pathways—and to use the pathways framework. One of the possible outcomes of such a culture—and one that seems to be most important to many policymakers—will be high student achievement. Dr. Comer constantly reminds us that students who develop well, learn well.

The Parent Team

One of the hallmarks of an effective school is the level of parent involvement. One of the three teams advocated within the SDP model for a high-functioning school is the Parent Team (PT). If the culture of the school is to be permeated by developmental understanding, parents and other caregivers must be a critical part of this effort. There needs to be a common language between the school and the home regarding the utilization of the pathways framework in all aspects of children's learning and development. The school, therefore, has a responsibility to educate parents and other caregivers about the importance of knowing children along these six pathways, and of the benefits of interacting with them from a developmental perspective. Parents should endeavor to

- use the pathways framework and language to share information with the school about their child's needs and concerns
- make a commitment to support the school's focus on the six pathways within the home and community
- ask the school staff to be explicit about how parents can support their efforts

Figure 4.3 Student and Staff Support Team student referral

Sample Referral Form for Student and Staff Support Team

_____
(school name)

Student: _____ Grade: _____ DOB: _____ Student # _____ Gender _____

Parent/Guardian/Surrogate: _____ Phone # (Work) _____ Phone # (Home) _____

Address: _____

Special Education? Y/N _____ Specify/Comment _____

Health Condition? Y/N _____ Specify/Comment _____

Medications? Y/N _____ Specify/Comment _____

Major Areas of Concerns: _____

Date of Referral: _____

Referral Source: _____ 504 Plan? Y/N ESOL? Y/N _____ Discipline Referrals? Y/N _____ Days Present _____

_____ (name/title) Days Absent _____

Developmental Pathways (Describe behaviors reflective of these pathways)	Describe Strengths	Describe Needs	Describe Current Interventions	Discussion Notes
Physical				
Cognitive				
Psychological				
Language				
Social				
Ethical				

SOURCE: Reprinted here courtesy of Prince George's County Comer Network, Maryland.

- with other members of the Parent Team, develop strategies that parents can use to support each other as they collectively and individually support the children along the pathways, for example

  make sure the child gets sufficient rest each night (physical pathway)

  use nonjudgmental language in discussions with and when disciplining the child (psychological and language pathways)

  encourage their child to complete homework each evening, and initiate conversations with the child about what is learned each day in school (cognitive and language pathways)

  make sure their actions are consistent with the message they want to convey about appropriate behaviors (social and ethical pathways)

When that common language is developed between home and school, and when common values are practiced and advocated by these two institutions, then the benefits can be substantial, particularly for the students. Dr. Comer (1988) captured this argument in his early writings:

> A child whose development meshes with the mainstream values encountered at school will be prepared to achieve at the level of his or her ability. In addition, the meshing of home and school fosters further development: when a child's social skills are considered appropriate by the teacher, they elicit positive reactions. A bond develops between the child and the teacher, who can now join in supporting the overall development of the child. (p. 45)

WORKING TOGETHER TO ENSURE THAT ALL CHILDREN DEVELOP TO THEIR FULL POTENTIAL

What is it that adults really want for children? Do they just want to raise or to teach "brains on sticks" who are extremely proficient performing at high levels on all achievement tests—and lack the ethical and social skills that demonstrate their humanity? Do they want to raise and to teach children who are well-adjusted—physically, cognitively, linguistically, ethically, socially, and psychologically—and who grow up to be adults who are positive, contributing members of society? If the latter is the preference, then the adults must make a deliberate effort to provide the needed and appropriate support to ensure children's learning, growth, and overall development. Quality development does not happen just by chance: It is continuously promoted through specific actions of adults. The activities and suggestions outlined in this chapter are not intended to be exhaustive. They are just the starting point. Everyone in a child's life contributes either positively or negatively to the child's development. This means that the school alone can't accomplish the job successfully; the home alone can't accomplish the job successfully; community-based services alone can't accomplish the job successfully. Successful learning and development depend on the ability of those institutions to share a common language, and work together collaboratively, to ensure that all children develop to their full potential and become productive and contributing citizens of the world.

REFERENCES

Berk, L. E. (1991). *Child development* (2nd ed.). Boston: Allyn & Bacon.

Comer, J. P. (1988). Educating poor minority children. *Scientific American, 259,* 42–48.

Erikson, E. (1963). *Childhood and society.* New York: Norton.

Maholmes, V. (2004). Designing the comprehensive school plan. In E. T. Joyner, M. Ben-Avie, & J. P. Comer, *Transforming school leadership and management to support student learning and development.* Thousand Oaks, CA: Corwin Press.

McLaughlin, M., Ennis, E., & Hernández, F. (2004). The school planning and management team: The engine that drives the school. In E. T. Joyner, M. Ben-Avie, & J. P. Comer, *Transforming school leadership and management to support student learning and development.* Thousand Oaks, CA: Corwin Press.

READ MORE ABOUT . . .

For information on the School Planning and Management Team, see "The School Planning and Management Team: The Engine That Drives the School," Chapter 3 in *Transforming School Leadership and Management to Support Student Learning and Development: The Field Guide to Comer Schools in Action* in this series.

For information on the Student and Staff Support Team, see "The Student and Staff Support Team and the Coordination of Student Services," Chapter 11 in *Transforming School Leadership and Management to Support Student Learning and Development: The Field Guide to Comer Schools in Action* in this series.

For information on parent involvement, see "Families as Partners," Chapter 10 in *Transforming School Leadership and Management to Support Student Learning and Development: The Field Guide to Comer Schools in Action* in this series.

For information on the Comprehensive School Plan, see "Designing the Comprehensive School Plan," Chapter 6 in *Transforming School Leadership and Management to Support Student Learning and Development: The Field Guide to Comer Schools in Action* in this series.

For a discussion of the application of the pathways in classrooms, see "Comer-in-the-Classroom," Chapter 6 in *Dynamic Instructional Leadership to Support Student Learning and Development: The Field Guide to Comer Schools in Action* in this series.

5

Promoting Youth Leadership Development in Comer Schools

Valerie Maholmes

The success of the Comer Process depends on how well the students understand its goals and live by its principles. It is important to instill that understanding and nurture that lifestyle. The school-based training activities and national leadership academies at Yale University detailed in this chapter promote students' development as leaders of their school communities. Students are thus preparing not only to be self-sustaining adults but also to participate proactively in the wider society. The School Development Program's (SDP) ultimate expression is in its graduates who—despite the challenges they may face—act to strengthen our democracy.

HOW FAR DO THE CHANGES REACH?

When students take responsibility for their development and for improving the school, then SDP's educational change initiative has truly worked. The role of the Comer Kids' Council is to help students learn about and manage their own development. We want students to be able to use the framework of child and youth development to help them make good decisions and good choices throughout their academic and adult lives. Moreover, we expect the students to focus not only on their own individual development, but also on their school's development. Students should not be passive bystanders in their own development and in school reform. School improvement is not a spectator sport.

"PROUD TO BE A COMER KID"

"Oh yes, I'm proud to be a Comer Kid, proud of who I am, proud of where I'm going, proud of what I'm doing. . . ." These are the words of the theme song for the National Comer Kids' Leadership Academy. Every year, this theme song and others are taught to youth around the country to engender a sense of national accord and pride among students attending schools in the Comer network. Research suggests that students who have a greater sense of belonging and identification with the school are more likely to persist and to adjust well to the school environment. For this reason, SDP created the National Comer Kids' Youth Development Program.

Comer Kids' Councils

Schools can turn their current student government association into Comer Kids' Councils in the same way that schools may modify their preexisting leadership teams under the guidance of the Comer Process.

A great deal of the focus of the Comer Kids' Council is on living the Comer Process. We want the students to know about representation. We want the students to understand the guiding principles of consensus, collaboration, and no-fault. We hope that the students will look at the issues within their school. We intend for them to use the data they collect to help promote academic learning. Along the way, we expect that students will take some ownership in improving the school and feel a sense of pride in the school.

Comer Kids' Leadership Academy

The highlight of the National Comer Kids' Youth Development Program is the Comer Kids' Leadership Academy, which brings together youth from across the country to instill in them a sense of belonging, and to make the youth aware that they are part of a national family of schools that attempts to foster the same kinds of values, skills, and beliefs in young people. We want the national leadership academies to provide students with the opportunity to have an experience outside of the limitations of the local environment and to meet other young people who are having the same issues and challenges, but who have learned to use the Comer Process to solve problems.

Since 1997, students from schools around the country have been coming to Yale as delegates to the Comer Kids' Leadership Academy. The goals of the academy are

- to promote student knowledge and understanding of the Comer Process
- to provide strategies and opportunities for students to be involved in SDP implementation
- to encourage students' responsibility for their own learning and development
- to promote parent involvement in student learning and development

- to inspire student motivation and persistence in school
- to build a national network of student leaders

More than 500 students have participated in the academy, and have returned to their schools with what they have learned. As a result, parents, school staffs, faith-based organizations, and universities have set up their own leadership academies in their school communities. What follows in this chapter are strategies and activities to promote youth leadership development in Comer schools.

THE COMER PROCESS FOR KIDS: WHAT STUDENTS SHOULD KNOW AND BE ABLE TO DO

Traditionally, implementation of the Comer Process has been guided by the adults in the building. The administration, staff, and parents set up the three teams and use the guiding principles to lead the school in planning for positive student developmental outcomes.

Staff development is provided continuously for new and veteran staff to ensure that the process reaches the institutional stage in the SDP Implementation Life Cycle. While the adults are learning the process and integrating the philosophy of the program into their ways of working, students also need opportunities to learn about the Comer Process and to begin implementing the Comer philosophy in their daily school life. Regardless of grade level, students who know about and understand the process are likely to be active contributors to a positive school climate, and to take responsibility for seeing that their school is a safe and inviting place to learn.

We use four standards for engaging students in the implementation process:

1. Students should know who Dr. Comer is and why he developed SDP.

2. Students should know about the six developmental pathways.

3. Students should know the guiding principles.

4. Students should know the goals in their school's Comprehensive School Plan.

STUDENTS SHOULD KNOW WHO DR. COMER IS AND WHY HE DEVELOPED SDP

Quite often students in Comer Schools may recognize new and exciting things happening in their school when the Comer Process is introduced, but if you ask them why their school has chosen the Comer Process, they might have a difficult time telling you. The students need to understand why the school has chosen to adopt the Comer model and what it means for them.

It is important for students to know that Dr. Comer was a young person whose life started with humble beginnings. He was able to become a world-renowned child psychiatrist because he had goals and dreams for himself. As a boy, Dr. Comer's parents and family guided him, and he worked hard and made positive choices that led to his success. He had three friends who were just as able academically as he was. His friends, on the other hand, did not have as much guidance and made life choices that were not as positive. As Dr. Comer grew older and decided to become a doctor, and as he thought about his friends, he eventually developed SDP as a way for adults to provide guidance so that students could be successful in school and in life.

The questions and activities below are used as an orientation for the National Comer Kids' Leadership Academy and can be adapted by teachers and school teams to teach kids about Dr. Comer. Other schools have designated Dr. Comer as a leader to be honored during Black History Month and have used these activities to introduce him to the student body.

Student Activity 5.1:
Dr. Comer is a child psychiatrist

This can be done as a writing activity or teachers can assign this as a research project.

Dr. James P. Comer is a very special man. He is a child psychiatrist.

What is a child psychiatrist?

_____

_____

_____

What does a child psychiatrist do?

_____

_____

_____

What did Dr. Comer have to do to become a child psychiatrist?

_____

_____

_____

Would you like to become a child psychiatrist?

_____

_____

_____

Student Activity 5.2: James's friends were not as successful as he was

This story can be told to students, or teachers can develop skits and let the students act out the roles.

When he was a boy, James P. Comer had three very close friends. They went to school together and played together after school. They were all very smart students, but as they grew older, only James continued to do well in school. His friends started having trouble in school. Eventually, they started doing bad things after school. James grew up to become a doctor and ultimately a world famous child psychiatrist. Unfortunately, his three friends were not so successful.

Write a story about Dr. Comer and his three friends. Use the questions below to create a different ending.

Why do you think Dr. Comer was able to be successful and his friends were not?

_____

_____

_____

What could his friends have done to have a better experience in school and in the community?

_____

_____

_____

What things could the teachers in the school have done to help James's friends do better in school?

_____

_____

_____

Student Activity 5.3: The members of the Comer teams work together to make good decisions for children

Students can interview teachers and parents to answer the questions in this activity.

When Dr. Comer became a child psychiatrist, he was asked to work in two schools in New Haven to help children who were having problems doing well in school. When he visited the schools, he found out that the schools were not very friendly places in which to teach and learn. He helped the adults in the schools and the parents work together better so that the schools could be much more exciting places for everyone. He organized three Comer teams—the School Planning and Management Team (SPMT), the Student and Staff Support Team (SSST), and the Parent Team (PT). These teams work together to make all the decisions in the school.

Does your school have these Comer teams?

_____

_____

_____

What are the Comer teams called in your school?

_____

_____

_____

What do these teams do?

_____

_____

_____

Can you name the teachers, parents, administrators, and others who are members of these teams?

_____

_____

_____

How do the Comer teams make your school a better place to teach and learn?

_____

_____

_____

STUDENTS SHOULD KNOW ABOUT THE SIX DEVELOPMENTAL PATHWAYS

The heart and soul of the Comer Process is its focus on healthy child development. The six pathways serve as an organizing framework for adults in decision making, lesson planning, and designing school programs. Many adults have indicated that learning about the pathways has empowered them in their teaching and in their child-rearing practices. Students, as well, need to know about their own development. They need to know what makes them whole beings, and how they can be happy, healthy, and successful in school and in life.

At the National Academy, student delegates are taught the language of development. They learn about each developmental pathway and how the pathways relate to each other. Finally, the students engage in a variety of activities that allow them to *experience* the pathways. The following are a few examples of how students can learn about the six pathways.

Student Activity 5.4: How do we grow up?

These definitions are suitable for ages 5–10. Older students can use the adult definitions in Chapter 4. Teachers can make posters illustrating the definitions of each pathway.

Pathways for Kids

Physical:	How our brains develop and how our bodies grow: The importance of health, nutrition, rest, and exercise
Language:	How we talk and how we listen
Psychological:	How we feel and what we think about ourselves
Ethical:	How we behave and how we follow rules
Social:	How we get along with each other and how we interact in different environments
Cognitive:	How we think and how we learn

Student Activity 5.5: Comercise! Social and physical pathways for young children

These activities were adapted and submitted by Mrs. Gayle Merritt, Mrs. Delores Varano, and Mrs. Betty Tursick at P.S. 19 in Paterson, New Jersey.

Comer Community

This activity promotes the social pathway. It can be conducted at the beginning of the year, or introduced as a way to greet children newly enrolled.

Give a brief explanation of the social pathway, and why it is important to get to know everyone. Then give the following directions:

For this activity, you will be working with a partner. When I give the signal, you will have five seconds to find your partner and introduce yourself. Then each pair must do the following as I call out the commands

Back to back!
Knee to knee!
Toe to toe!
Heel to heel!
Shoulder to shoulder!
Elbow to elbow!

On the final command, "People to people," find a new partner and we'll start the fun all over again.

At the end of the activity, ask children how it felt to participate in the activity, and to meet other children in this way.

Comer Current/Circuit

This activity can be modified for students of all ages. It can be utilized during gym or structured recess time.

Organize the students into a large circle. Have students hold hands with each other. Place a large Hoola Hoop on the forearm of one of the students in the circle. Direct each child in the circle to step through the hoop without breaking the circle or letting go of the hands.

After a couple of rounds add an additional hoop.

When the activity is completed, lead students in a discussion about the ways in which they had to help each other to get the task accomplished.

Comer Corral

This activity supports the physical pathway for young children by giving them the opportunity to strengthen their gross motor abilities and physical coordination. It can be used to introduce new topics or curriculum themes.

Spread 8 to 10 hoops randomly in an open area. Play appropriate music for movement. Instruct children to go around the hoops in various modes of movement (skipping, hopping, walking, etc.).

When the music stops, students must get into a hoop on command. No more than three or four students can be in a hoop at any time. Ask students to introduce themselves. You can then ask students in one hoop to recite the days of the week or any curriculum theme you might be introducing for the week.

All of these activities can be adapted for elementary and middle school students. For high school students, teachers can review the pathways at the beginning of the year, and ask students to set goals along each of the pathways for themselves and for the class as a whole. Then, let the students create journals organized according to the pathways to chart their progress. Each student should expect to share at least one journal entry during the course of the year. The class as a whole can check in on a weekly basis to see how they are working together toward the goals.

STUDENTS SHOULD KNOW THE THREE GUIDING PRINCIPLES, THE "COMER GOLDEN RULES FOR CLASSROOM INTERACTION"

Other chapters in this book focus on the importance of positive relationships and the guiding principles of consensus, collaboration, and no-fault problem solving. Students in Comer schools need to know that relationships, a positive school climate, and a positive classroom climate are central foci of SDP.

Relationships help promote students' development socially and psychologically, and they help to create an atmosphere in the classroom that allows students to perform at optimal levels. Therefore students need to know that collaboration and teamwork are expected of everyone in the school. In addition, students need to know that they will have opportunities to reach consensus on important class decisions. During their discussions they will be expected to honor the guiding principle of no-fault problem solving.

Student Activity 5.6: Teamwork is important

The following guiding questions are used at the National Academy to prepare students for working in teams. These were shared by Mrs. Linda Lett-Nugroho from Prince George's County, Maryland.

Dr. Comer says teamwork is important. We must cooperate when we work on a team.

What kinds of teams are you a part of?

_____

_____

_____

What kind of teamwork do you do at home?

_____

_____

_____

What have you learned from being on a team?

_____

_____

_____

What does it take for teams to be effective?

_____

_____

_____

Student Activity 5.7:
Open lunch—Problem solving
using all three guiding principles

This problem-solving activity gives students the opportunity to utilize all three of the guiding principles. This activity was submitted by Mrs. June Eckardt at P.S. 25 in Paterson, New Jersey, in response to issues raised by her middle school students.

Open lunch is defined as students being permitted to leave the school grounds during their lunch period. Considering the times in which we live, should middle school students be permitted to have an open lunch? Have students choose a position and be ready to defend it with at least three solid reasons.

Students work in teams of three or four to tackle this problem. They brainstorm a list of ideas and examine the pros and cons of each idea. Using the consensus process, each team pares the list down to its best three explanations and shares those ideas with the other teams.

The class selects the best ideas from each of the teams and reaches consensus to answer the question. The teacher leads the class in an open discussion about the process and outcomes of the activity.

Any topic can be used in this process. Students should be instructed to respect all contributions made to the process and to find the best solution to the problem without demeaning other students.

STUDENTS SHOULD KNOW
THE GOALS IN THEIR SCHOOL'S
COMPREHENSIVE SCHOOL PLAN

Just as students need to feel a sense of belonging and connection to others, they also need to feel a sense of allegiance to their school. They need to take responsibility for helping the school become a good place to learn. Sharing with students the broad goals in the Comprehensive School Plan helps students understand why the school staff has chosen to implement certain programs, policies, and practices.

Planning for Success

By sharing this information, the adults in the school model for students the concept that to become successful one must set feasible goals, establish a plan, assess, and modify. Students should be aware of school-level data such as overall attendance rates, achievement level, and school climate. Students can participate in the planning process by generating their own data and by making recommendations to the SPMT. (For decision-making process, see Student Activity 5.8 and Figure 5.1.) The more students know about the planning process, the better able they are to make meaningful contributions to the school's overall improvement efforts.

Figure 5.1   Weighing in the balance worksheet

Consensus means we solve problems by talking and sharing how we feel until we find a solution everyone will support.

Problem we want to solve at our school:
_____

Possible solutions:
_____

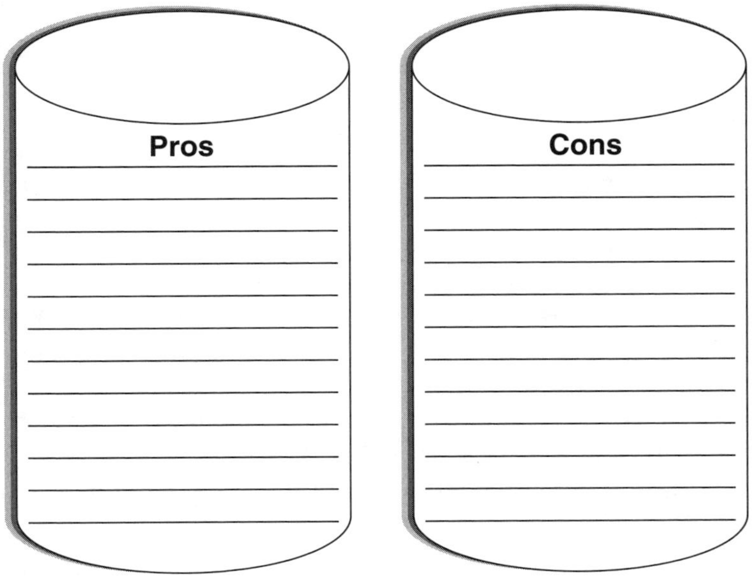

_____

Pros

Cons

Student Activity 5.8:
A lesson in effective decision making

Purpose/Objectives

The purpose of this lesson is to provide students with an opportunity to reflect on the importance of effective decision making as a fundamental skill for success in school and in life. Students participating in this exercise will

- learn to think critically about handling the challenges that confront them
- learn to solve problems on their own using a problem-solving framework
- seek support and guidance for decisions that may be too complex for them to manage

Participants: This lesson is best suited for students in Grades 6 through 10, but can be adapted for other students

Materials: Weighing in the Balance worksheet (Figure 5.1)

Time: Approximately 40–50 minutes

Directions:

Whole class discussion/warm-up (10 minutes):

- Review with the students the importance of making effective decisions.
- Share examples of the types of decisions that we make on a daily basis.
- Lead a discussion on the types of decisions and choices students make regularly (e.g., where to eat, what to wear).
- Focus discussion on the kinds of decisions that have an impact on our lives (e.g., to come to school regularly, to study/work hard, to engage in bad behavior, to choose certain friends).

Small group activity (20 minutes):

- Break students into small groups of two or three.
- Have each group select a notetaker and a reporter.
- Hand out the Weighing in the Balance worksheet (Figure 5.1).
- Ask students to share with one another problems that they are currently encountering.
- Students will use the worksheet to brainstorm and discuss the pros and cons of potential strategies for resolving the problems.
- When each group has finished, the reporter will share the potential strategies that the group discussed.

Whole group report-outs (15 minutes):

- The reporter from each group will share the group's worksheet.
- The session leader will jot down key themes gleaned from each student presentation.

Summary and closure (10 minutes):

- At the end of the presentations, discuss the themes.
- Lead the group in a discussion regarding decision-making strategies, weighing the pros and cons, and seeking adult support when decisions seem too complex.
- Respond to questions and answers.

SETTING UP A COMER KIDS' COUNCIL

Getting Started

Once the students have a basic understanding of the Comer Process, it's time to get them involved! As is the case with the overall SDP implementation, setting up governance and management processes to foster collaborative decision making is an important first step in getting youth leadership development programs up and running. Many schools already have student government and youth councils, which can easily be transformed into Comer Kids' Councils.

Purpose of the Council

The purpose of the Comer Kids' Council is to promote leadership among the students in the school. Utilizing the Comer guiding principles and the six developmental pathways as a framework, students will become skilled at taking responsibility for their own learning, development, and behavior. They will learn four essential skills of leadership—modeling good behavior, decision making, problem solving, and achievement motivation. The ultimate goal of the council is to improve or enhance student academic performance by directly involving students in decision making on issues that affect their interest and engagement in school.

Role of the Council

The council is supervised by the SPMT and functions as a student branch of the SPMT. The council integrates the Comer guiding principles and team roles during meetings. Utilizing action research strategies, council members identify at least one critical issue that they will address during the academic year. Then they collect, analyze, and report data to the SPMT, as well as develop an action plan. The findings from the needs assessment and action plan should be incorporated into the comprehensive school planning process and should be posted on the Comer Kids' Bulletin Board.

Team Meetings

The council meets at least twice each month at a time designated by the SPMT. Students should select roles (chair, facilitator, notekeeper, reporter, liaison) to facilitate the meeting process. Selected council representatives (the chair and liaison) attend SPMT meetings at least quarterly. Selected delegates may also attend a specially planned PT or SSST meeting if student input is needed to address a particular issue.

Relationship to Classroom Practice

The SPMT should strive to integrate certain activities of the Comer Kids' Council into classroom practice. These activities should be aligned with the instructional goals, and enhance the academic focus and achievement motivation of the students. Staff development should be provided to assist in classroom integration.

Selection of Student Representatives to the Council

Students are selected by their peers to serve on the council. This is important so that students can begin to learn how to *represent* their constituents—an expectation of members of the School Planning and Management Team. Schools may use a variety of selection processes, including a process of consensus, run-offs by grade level, student debates, and essay contests. The goal, however, is that the students understand that they represent their peers. They may also have the opportunity to represent their school at the district-level academy, or possibly act as delegates at the National Leadership Academy at Yale. Once students are selected, they must attend an orientation that helps strengthen their understanding of the goals and objectives of the Comer Process.

Composition of the Comer Kids' Leadership Council

- student representatives selected by their peers, starting at the fourth-grade level (total number to be determined by the SPMT)

- a representative from the SSST (e.g., guidance counselor, school psychologist, social worker)

- a representative from the Comer Parent Team

- a representative from the SPMT

- a representative from the school Administrative Team (principal, assistant principal, etc.)

SPMT Roles and Responsibilities for the Council

The SPMT has the primary responsibility for shepherding the process of developing student leadership. The following is a sampling of the roles and responsibilities assigned to the SPMT to ensure that the Comer Kids' Council is fully implemented and becomes an integral part of school life:

- Establish and supervise a Comer Kids' Leadership Council.

- Establish policy guidelines for school programs and youth leadership development activities.

- Carry out systematic school planning related to academics, child development, school climate, staff development, youth leadership, and public relations.

- Plan an annual calendar that integrates academic, social, staff, and youth leadership development functions.

- Assist Comer Kids' Council with conducting student needs assessment and identifying the priority issue(s) the council will address during the academic year.

- Create a Comer Kids' bulletin board that displays the process and outcomes of the council's activities.

ENCOURAGING STUDENTS' RESPONSIBILITY FOR THEIR OWN LEARNING AND DEVELOPMENT

In our efforts to promote school improvement, we often overlook the important contributions that students can make. Students are keenly aware of what is working well and not working so well in their school, but we rarely provide a forum for students to share what they know. Similarly, students also have an intuitive sense about the approaches to learning that are working well or not so well for them. Although they may not have the language to articulate their thoughts or efficient strategies to overcome some of their learning difficulties, students want to be successful in school. The Comer Kids' Council can be a wonderful resource for establishing peer tutoring and mentoring programs. Town hall meetings led by council members can also be an exciting way to give voice to students' ideas, issues, and concerns about school improvement.

PROMOTING PARENT INVOLVEMENT IN YOUTH DEVELOPMENT: "I TOO HAVE A DREAM"

Without parent involvement, it is impossible to have a successful youth leadership development program. We have heard many times that parents are the child's first teachers. They also provide the child with his or her first examples of leadership. Children observe and adopt the leadership styles of their parents—how they make decisions, listen and interact with other adults, and how they solve problems. Maggie Comer, Dr. Comer's mother, was a wonderful example of how parents, regardless of educational limitations, family background, or economic status, can play a critical role in supporting their children's development.

During the academic year, the Parent Team should host an orientation for all parents so that they can be introduced to the basic principles of child development, and learn ways in which they can foster and support the healthy development of their children. Reading circles for parents featuring copies of *Maggie's American Dream* are a great way to foster discussions about dreams for themselves and their children. At the National Leadership Academy, parent chaperones are asked to write down their dreams (see Figure 5.2). At the end of the academy, the parents read them aloud to their children.

Figure 5.2   Parents, too, have dreams for themselves and their children

BUILDING CAPACITY THROUGH STUDENT LEADERSHIP

Setting Up Your Own Leadership Academy

While many of the activities described in this chapter are taken from the Comer Kids' Leadership Academy at Yale, they can be easily adapted and implemented at a district-level youth academy. Establishing a local Comer Kids' Leadership Academy will allow a district to build capacity among the student leadership, thereby promoting prosocial behavior and establishing positive student models across grade levels and school sites.

Pre-Academy Activities

Delegates from each school are selected by their peers to represent their school at the district academy. (Typically delegates are Comer Kids' Council members.) The delegates have several tasks to complete before participating in the academy. In fact, the academy should be the culminating event, not the beginning of the students' involvement in the Comer Process. Delegates are introduced to the Comer Kids' theme songs that will be performed at the academy. Delegates are also asked to attend at least two SPMT meetings and to identify an issue that they and their constituents would like to have addressed by their peers at the academy. With the support and guidance of adult SPMT members, the student delegates clarify the issue of interest that they will be sharing at the district academy.

The Trip to the Academy

Delegates and their chaperones travel to the academy site (usually a campsite or a local college) from various places across the district—some by train, and others by bus, car, or plane. For many students this is their first time away from home. It is highly recommended that the delegate teams take this opportunity to make geography, social studies, and other aspects of the school curricula come alive. We encourage participating schools to adapt the following "travel curriculum." Students have the opportunity to learn a great deal as they travel, and by engaging students with these contests and activity sheets, parents and chaperones help to alleviate fear of travel and feelings of homesickness.

Student Activity 5.9: Sample travel curriculum for an academy meeting

Packing Up and Getting Ready to Go!

Give students, parents, and chaperones a checklist for packing and preparing for the trip. In addition to clothing items, sundries, and other necessities, the checklist should include several zip-type plastic bags, three-by-five index cards, markers, a journal, and a disposable camera. The latter items will help students collect information and record events along their journey.

Getting on Board!

Whatever the mode of travel, departure is probably the most exciting time of the trip. The air is filled with excitement and anticipation about the trip. Yet due to the new security procedures, there may also be extensive wait time. To ensure students' safety and to maintain their enthusiasm, have students sit together in small groups and take out their markers and three-by-five index cards. Ask each group to write down all the travel related words and phrases they see in the immediate vicinity. Collect all the cards and hold onto them for later.

And Away We Go!

After everyone is seated, have the students take out their journals to write down their feelings, thoughts, and ideas about the trip. What do they see, feel, and experience that is different? Solicit the cooperation of the attendants on the bus, plane, or train to help carry out the travel activities.

About halfway through the trip, consult the index cards on which students wrote while waiting to depart. If riding a chartered bus, play a game of charades and have students act out the words. Or play the "sentence infinity" game. Start a sentence using one of the words on the card. Have a student volunteer choose a card, and then add to the sentence using the selected card. Continue until all words have been used in sentences.

Here at Last!

Upon approaching the academy site, remind students to take pictures and to write in their journals daily about what they see, hear, and experience that is the same or different from what they experience back home. Have them use plastic bags to collect interesting items they find during their stay. On the trip back home, take a moment to have students share their findings.

Academy Agenda and Activities

The National Comer Kids' Academy lasts for four days in the summer. Districts can shorten or lengthen the duration of the academy depending on the ages of the students and their program goals.

The first evening of the academy is devoted to building community and developing relationships. Just as in the adult 101 or 102 academies, student delegates from each school lead their fellow delegates in an introductory community-building activity that they have prepared. This allows students to be introduced to one another in a fun and nonthreatening way. Then, students are randomly assigned to groups so that for the remainder of the academy they have the opportunity to meet and work with delegates from other schools.

On each day of the academy, the students learn, in practical terms, how to facilitate continued improvement with aspects of the Comer Process when they return to their home schools. They focus on the guiding principles by engaging in a variety of group activities, at the end of which they process what they have learned and discuss how it felt to work in a group. They strengthen their knowledge of the developmental pathways by playing board games and other activities that promote the use of developmental language. To learn about consensus, they participate in role-playing activities that help them learn the difference between consensus decision making and voting. They also experiencce how important it is for them to take active roles in decision-making activities back home. During this time, students share the issues they have brought from their respective SPMTs and receive ideas and feedback from their peers.

On the last day of the Comer Kids' Academy, students and chaperones do back-home planning together. In this activity, the delegates have the opportunity to teach the adults and lead them in discussion. Parents and teachers typically ask students what can be done to involve students with the Comer Process in their school, and how they can help students become more inspired to work to their full potential. Parents take the opportunity to read their dreams statements to their children.

The Academy Awards

The highlight of the trip is the Academy Awards Dinner. During the course of the academy, parents and chaperones observe student interaction and reach consensus on three students who will each receive a Guiding Principles Award. The delegates nominate a student from their working group to receive the James P. Comer

Leadership Award. The selection process for this award begins with group facilitators leading students in a discussion about leadership. The facilitators list and discuss the leadership qualities of Dr. Comer. Finally, students are asked to nominate someone from their group to receive the award and to write persuasive arguments to support their candidate for the award. Once all the nominations are received, the group facilitators meet to discuss the nominations, make the final selections, and seal the names in an envelope to be presented at the awards dinner. School districts can choose to introduce other award categories, such as a Superintendent's Award. All students receive a certificate of participation.

Post-Academy Activities

When school starts in the fall, teachers and chaperones are expected to continue involving academy delegates in roles of leadership. Students need to be able to take on leadership roles in the school so that they, with the guidance and support of the adults in the school, can put into practice some of the ideas they developed during the summer. This is also an important responsibility for the SPMT and the PT to assume.

POSITIVE OUTCOMES AND PROFOUND IMPACT

The Comer Kids' Academy has had a profound impact on the students who have participated and on their home schools and districts. Our aim is to make sure that students have more than just a nice trip to an academy site—that they use the experience as a basis from which they learn to take responsibility for their own learning and development. A delegate from one of our most recent academies tells the story of her experience at a Comer Kids' Academy in the essay that follows.

Student Essay: "What it meant to become a Comer Kid"

"What it meant to become a Comer Kid"

Hi, my name is Jasmine Ortiz. Last summer I attended the Comer Kids' Academy. Students from New Haven, New York, and Virginia attended this academy. The kids were all different ages and in the third through eighth grade. That was the first time I really heard anything about Dr. Comer. We all participated in lots of activities that had to do with helping our schools. We listened and discussed these problems and we all tried to come up with solutions.

All the kids I met were just like me, a Comer Kid. We were all working with Comer's guiding principles, which are collaboration, consensus, and no-fault. Collaboration is when everyone shares their ideas; consensus, that's when the group or class makes a decision, and no-fault is if someone doesn't get the answer right, it's not their fault and we do not laugh.

When I went back to school my class made a big puzzle and every piece had a characteristic of a Comer Kid. We created the list together and fit the pieces together as a team. It was fun! My teacher, Mrs. Savenelli, decided to make a program called the Dream Team. Our government has second, third and fourth graders. We are young leaders selected by our teachers. When it was close to Thanksgiving we made posters to remind everyone at Martin Luther King School to bring in as many cans and boxes as possible. We did so well and brought the food to the Dixwell Community House. They were very happy.

The older kids always talk to the classes with a younger team member about our activities. It helps us speak. We also scheduled a time and date around Christmas and went to STOP SHOP. Everyone helped to make this happen. We held our board up, asked people to give us money and asked if they could buy some food in the store. It was like a miracle in three hours! We gave turkeys and hams and food to ten of our school families.

We had an all school movie day and bagged over 200 bags of popcorn. We are having two more spirit days this spring. The Dream Team has printed stationery to bring to the nursing home. We will be working with old people a lot.

The other two kids that came to Dr. Comer's academy are leading the Dream Team with me in dance routines about our education. It is so exciting! We are going to dance at our fashion show and march in the Freddy Fixer Parade.

If I never went to this great academy, these new experiences would not be happening to me. I would have missed out on that wonderful and great educational academy. No one knew each other, but we shared and we laughed and we worked like friends with respect.

Thank you, Dr. Comer and Mrs. Savenelli.

Children Must Be Taught to Deal With Anger

Yale Child Study Center Faculty

If you need to convince people that social and emotional health are prerequisites for academic learning, point to the scarring effects on students and staff of emotional and physical violence in and around schools. The problem may seem insurmountable, yet leading authorities maintain that teaching families, schools, and police about child and adolescent development produces immediate and lifelong benefits. The article reprinted here can bolster proposals for ongoing training in anger management and healthy relationships.

Recent events have riveted national attention on children and teenagers who threaten or commit acts of violence. Schools—once considered safe and protected environments—have emerged as places of heightened fear and suspicion. Paradoxically, while death from injury accounts for about 75 percent of all deaths of teenagers, murder is a very, very uncommon act perpetrated by children younger than 18.

Ironically, part of the tremendous media exposure for such events is motivated by their extreme rarity. The combination of media coverage and the inherent repugnance

---

NOTE: Adapted from an article originally published in the *New Haven Register*, May 26, 1999. Reprinted with permission from the *New Haven Register*.

of such acts of violence capture public attention. In this way, people easily develop gross misperceptions about children who kill. These include powerful stereotypes that suggest: All children are inherently dangerous; any child can inexplicably turn murderous; adults have no influence over the development of violent behavior in children; the larger community and society are either completely responsible or completely free of any responsibility for children who murder.

SIGNS OF TROUBLE

Although our scientific understanding of why such events occur is still quite elementary, we know some things for certain. Children who murder usually display a complex history of dangerous behaviors and experiences. These essential elements include relentless exposure to direct or vicarious violence, alienation from healthy peer and community relationships, lack of appropriate parental and other adult supervision, and progressive escalation of obvious antisocial behaviors.

Anger and aggression are powerful and universal emotions from infancy throughout life. For most children and adolescents, aggressive impulses are channeled into positive behaviors and constructive activities that lead to healthy and productive adulthood. For others, a complex interaction of family, individual, and environmental factors may lead to more violent and deviant behavior.

When the institutions important to children—such as family, schools, and police—share an understanding of child and adolescent development, the possibility of promoting healthy patterns of behavior is increased. Understanding and responding to the important issues of the primary development phases from infancy through adolescence will help us move our children on the path away from violence toward health.

INFANTS AND YOUNG CHILDREN

A baby or young child's ability to manage his or her aggressive feelings depends on a number of factors such as a growing ability to substitute thought for action. Children learn to use words rather than to hit to get what they want. Normal strivings for independence and assertiveness are dealt with in a social context from the first weeks of life and become readily observable as the capacity for speech expands and the motor ability to move away from parents increases.

The push toward independence and assertiveness comes into view even more sharply as parents and others begin to make greater demands of the child, asking the child to delay his need for immediate gratification and to develop more self-control. Parents often report that disputes over aggression are particularly dramatic at this age when children realize they have the capacity for independence.

As time goes on, children learn a number of ways to deal with their aggressive feelings. Some of this learning is rather obvious, direct, and explicit, like being told, "Johnny don't hit—ask your brother for the toy." However, an even greater part of how the child learns is less open and explicit. In fact, much of infant and toddler learning comes from the careful observation of parents and other important adults and the ways in which they deal with their own anger and aggression.

This is a particularly critical issue for younger children because it implies that even more than what parents say, what they actually do influences the child's behavior.

Children who are exposed to aggression are more likely to think of it as an appropriate response. Parents who punish their children more frequently and severely have children who are more likely to behave more aggressively. Exposure of children to aggression from other sources such as television also may contribute to their violent behavior.

SCHOOL-AGE CHILDREN

By the time children are finishing elementary school and entering middle school, they are usually equipped with fairly sturdy mechanisms to help them cope with everyday life.

If all goes well, they have age-appropriate skills. They have learned to get along with their peers and to attend to their work. They have interests and hobbies and a fair amount of respect and admiration for the adults in their lives. They have learned to cope with anger, disappointment, and sadness as well as positive emotions so that they are not overwhelmed. They have gained a sense of competence, knowledge of right and wrong, and they feel pretty good about themselves.

Perhaps most important, they have a sense of humor and trust the world around them. They are beginning to feel prepared for life. That is, if all has gone well around them. If all has not gone well and these ingredients have not been present, chances are children will not feel good about themselves, will not be able to modulate strong negative emotions, will not trust the adult world, and will lack a sense of future and of right and wrong.

Poverty, violence, and family instability may exacerbate their problems. In addition, the vulnerability of all children increases with a lack of appropriate parental supervision and engagement, few positive adult role models, access to inappropriate media, and the availability of guns. Many troubled children do not receive the services that might help them. In the United States, two-thirds of all children with mental health needs do not receive any help. Children counseled in schools or clinics have, in most cases, improved behavior, improved grades, and have returned to a healthier developmental course.

ADOLESCENCE

At least since biblical times, writers have agreed that the transition from childhood to adulthood is a time of emotional and behavioral turmoil. Physical changes, along with sexual and aggressive urges, accelerate all at once in a way never again duplicated, and they hit the teenager before there is a comparable spurt in mature judgment. If this volatile mix were not difficult enough, there are the added social expectations for teenagers to prepare for a future job or career and to form their own adult identity.

Some rebellion is normal during adolescence. It is necessary to learn who one is as separate from one's parents and to take one's place in forming the new generation. The task for the older generation is to help teenagers find their individuality without hurting themselves or others.

About three-quarters of the deaths of teenagers 15–19 are due to motor vehicle accidents, homicides, and suicides. The two immediate factors for most of these deaths, often found together in homicide and suicide, are alcohol and guns. If ways to smooth teenagers' inherently difficult biological, psychological, and social tasks were easy, the problem would not still be so painful after thousands of years. On the other hand, each generation has a duty to do better by its children than did the last.

Box 6.1 Ways to Cope With Youth Violence

- The media, particularly the visual media, should stop emphasizing youth violence. Studies are clear that the repeated viewing of violence makes it more acceptable to teens.
- Schools need an easy and confidential way for students to obtain mental health services.
- Parents, police, and the community as a whole must enforce rigorous alcohol and other drug laws.
- Families must not buy handguns. Statistics show they are more likely to cause a homicide or suicide than a criminal's death.

AUTHORS' NOTE: The Yale Child Study Center faculty who contributed to this chapter were Jean Adnopoz, associate clinical professor; Paula Armbruster, associate clinical professor; Steven Berkowitz, M.D., assistant professor; James Comer, M.D., associate dean and professor of psychiatry; Steven Marans, assistant professor of child psychoanalysis; John Schowalter, M.D., professor of child psychiatry; Fred Volkmar, M.D., associate professor of child psychiatry, pediatrics, and psychology; and Joseph Woolston, M.D., associate professor of pediatrics.

7

Children With Special Needs

Special Education and the Comprehensive School Plan

Michael Ben-Avie, Virginia Arrington, Morton Frank, and Robert Raymond

We asked Dr. Comer where, specifically, special education fits into the Comer Process. Does special education function as if it were a subcommittee of the Student and Staff Support Team? He replied, "Of course. More important, however, is the need to recognize that in our fragmented educational system, such programs as special education, bilingual education, and regular education tend to exist side by side in the same building without any contact with each other." He told us that it is critical that the goals and objectives of special education be incorporated into each school's Comprehensive School Plan and become "owned" by the whole school community. These goals and objectives also have to align with local, state, and national academic and developmental standards. In this chapter, the authors describe a school district that recently unified itself in this way.

SCHOOLWIDE PREVENTIVE PLANNING

Special education teachers and paraprofessionals know what it takes to be strong advocates for children. What they may not recognize, however, is that continuously operating in a crisis mode can sap their reservoir of perseverance. And without perseverance, daily frustrations will get in their way as they try to help children. When the classroom blinds won't open, when their best friend leaves the school, when a new procedure has to be implemented—it is during these times that a well-functioning school community can make all the difference. Within well-functioning school communities, everyone is aware of the federal and state regulations that impact most aspects of the special education classroom. When the school community designs its Comprehensive School Plan, the goals and objectives of the school's special education program are considered in tandem with those of such other school programs as bilingual and regular education. Schoolwide preventive planning helps staff move out of the crisis mode.

When school districts or schools are operating in a crisis mode, staff tend to focus only on their own concerns; they feel that they do not have the energy to do anything beyond their day-to-day work. The "comprehensive" in "comprehensive planning" is used here in the broadest sense possible to encompass staff as well as students. Operating in a problem-solving mode (as opposed to a crisis mode), staff are able to experience successes. This is because staff develop reasonable plans with clear, measurable goals and objectives. Staff align these goals and objectives with appropriate strategies. The outcome measures are clearly aligned with these strategies. When this system is working, staff diagnose well, prescribe well, and check often.

CREATING A UNIFIED EDUCATIONAL SYSTEM

A Districtwide Comprehensive School Plan for CSD 17

Up until the most recent school system restructuring in 2003, Community School District (CSD) 17 in Brooklyn, New York, had a single comprehensive plan that encompassed both regular and special education throughout the district—with one system of accountability.

Before the creation of the unified educational system, the schools reported to the district office, and the Committee on Special Education and the school-based support teams reported to the city's central Board of Education. The central board controlled the budget, hiring, clinical services, and instruction. The district housed the Committee on Special Education, but everything was done from NYC's central office.

When the Committee on Special Education was placed under the jurisdiction of CSD 17, Superintendent Evelyn Castro conducted a marriage ceremony, a real ceremony that even included the throwing of rice. The thrust of the marriage was that everyone would work as one team, with everybody on the same page at the same time doing whatever was necessary for the benefit of the children.

Consensus, Collaboration, and No-fault Problem Solving

In 1968, when Comer, as head of a Yale Child Study Center team, intervened in two New Haven schools, he realized that it was not enough just to bring together all those who had a stake in the lives of the students. The stakeholders needed guiding principles for their discussions. The three guiding principles of the Comer Process are consensus, collaboration, and no-fault. In Community School District 17, the no-fault guiding principle has been invaluable.

In a fault-seeking and fault-finding school climate, people are afraid of being blamed, and they have a tendency to point their finger at someone else and say, "Well, that one told me to do it." In contrast, the Comer Process atmosphere of no-fault removes the fear of being blamed, and people start to accept responsibility for positive outcomes instead of looking for ways to escape responsibility for negative outcomes. The no-fault and collaboration principles of the Comer Process also help to bring together people who otherwise would not be on the same team: social workers, psychologists, teachers, principals, assistant principals, security guards, school aides, custodians, and the lunchroom staff. (Some children act out only in the lunchroom. Who is in a better position to provide information about what these children do than the lunchroom staff?) That's what the Comer Process is about. *Everybody* plays a part in helping each child progress.

REGULAR EDUCATION EARLY INTERVENTION TEAMS

Collaborative Problem Solving and the Home-School Collaboration

Collaborative problem solving and the home-school collaboration are ways of using all resources *before* referring children to special education. CSD 17 doesn't even use the term *prereferral* anymore because that assumes an intervention that will eventually lead to special education. Instead, district staff set up regular education early intervention teams that involve all those who have a stake in the life success of the children. This "whole school" approach to solving problems is the closest intersection with the Comer Process.

Regular Education Early Intervention Teams known as Pupil Personnel Teams (PPTs) were piloted throughout CSD 17 in 1994. The PPTs discuss ways to solve the issue at hand, and they set up and carry out action plans with measurable outcomes. As of 2000–2001, PPTs were functioning in all the district schools. As a result, the referral rate decreased dramatically.

> You don't necessarily want special education: You want relief and the problem to be solved.

District superintendent Castro emphasized that each school relies on its regular education early intervention team. Each team consists of regular and special education staff, an administrator, the guidance counselor, and anyone else who wants to attend. In her September 5, 2002, memorandum to all staff members, Castro wrote: "The Pupil Personnel Team (PPT) in your school must be used to examine why an individual student is demonstrating significant academic, social, or physical needs, and then to develop support strategies and services in a non–special education setting."

PPTs are infused with the ideas of collaborative problem solving and the home-school collaboration. One of the ways in which one of the authors, Morton Frank, supervisor of school psychologists, persuades principals to adopt collaborative problem solving and home-school collaboration is by saying to them, "You don't necessarily want special education: You want relief and the problem to be solved."

The PPT Process

In CSD 17, the PPT process works in this manner:

1. The teacher or another school staff member gives the name of the child to a member of the PPT. The PPT facilitator, that child's case manager on the PPT, uses a consultation form (Figure 7.1) and a tracking form (Figure 7.2) to record data.

2. PPT members share knowledge of the student, and the facilitator assigns a Behavioral Assessment/Behavior Intervention Plan (BA/BIP) coordinator for each student. The BA/BIP coordinator is a member of the PPT.

3. The BA/BIP coordinator then meets with the teacher and other involved personnel. Forms on which to document behaviors and incidents, and strategies designed to deal with them, are distributed to school personnel by the BA/BIP coordinator.

4. After a two-week period, the BA/BIP coordinator collects these forms and meets with the teacher(s), the guidance counselor, and members of the school-based support team (school social worker, school psychologist, and educator evaluator). Collectively, they analyze the forms, and a Behavior Intervention Plan is drawn up for the student.

5. The BA/BIP coordinator meets with the parents, teacher(s), and student to discuss the plan and its implementation. This meeting is conducted in a fact-finding and problem-solving mode. Here's where the Comer Process comes in: There's equal responsibility, and there's no blame. Everyone is trained to say, "There is no blame. No matter what you see. People are doing the best that they can, given their resources and given the circumstances." The plan is signed by all parties.

6. The plan is disseminated to all adults in the school by the BA/BIP coordinator, who monitors the plan's effectiveness through periodic follow-ups. The BA/BIP coordinator makes sure that everyone who is involved with that child has a copy of the plan. For example, if there's a problem in the lunchroom, someone has to document on the incident log what triggered the behavior in that context. Everyone's looking for the fancy dynamics within the child, but we often find that the fancy dynamics are in the interactions between the child and his or her everyday environment.

> After a while, we ask the parents, "Do you still want your child tested for special education services?" and they say, "What for?" because the problem is solved.

This process works. We put our best efforts into it, and after a while we ask the parents, "Do you still want your child tested for special education services?" and they say, "What for?" because the problem is solved.

Figure 7.1 Community School District 17 facilitator's consultation form

Facilitator's Consultation Form

Student's Name _____ **Class** _____

Facilitator's Name _____ **Date Assigned** _____

1. Is there a discrepancy between student's academic skills and those skills necessary for the current setting?

2. What is the student's learning style? Are current instructional methods meeting student's needs? If not, explain.

3. Describe student's social and emotional characteristics (mood, ability to work independently, frustration tolerance, attention span, etc.).

4. How does the student relate to peers and adults? Please describe.

5. What, if any, community or family issues may be impacting the student's functioning in school?

(Continued)

Figure 7.1 (Continued)

6. Describe significant events in family.

7. Describe student's attitudes, concerns, etc.

8. Additional pertinent information

Outcome of the Consultation:

_____ Issue satisfactorily resolved   Date _____

_____ Recommendation for PPT intervention   Date _____

Facilitator's Signature

Figure 7.2   Community School District 17 Pupil Personnel Team intervention tracking form

Pupil Personnel Team Intervention Tracking Form, School Year _____

Student's Name	Class	Referring Source	Facilitator's Name	Date to PPT	Disposition Date	Comments

SOURCE: Courtesy of New York City Community School District 17. Reprinted from *Six Pathways to Healthy Child Development and Academic Success: The Field Guide to Comer Schools in Action*, by James P. Comer, Edward T. Joyner, and Michael Ben-Avie. Reproduction authorized only for the local school site that has purchased this book. www.corwinpress.com.

USING CONTRACTS TO HELP STUDENTS UNDERSTAND CHOICES AND CONSEQUENCES

What do you do for a truant? Well, someone has to sit down and find out what's going on. Are there stresses at home? Is the parent a working parent not at home to supervise? What is the role of peer pressure? Usually, we can solve the problem. In rare cases, the underlying problem is severe neglect and we must involve the Administration of Children's Services. If the only intervention for a severely neglected child is to put him into special education, no progress is going to be made.

Behavior Intervention Plans

The consequences written into a Behavior Intervention Plan have to be delivered *by the home*, not just by the school. Without having a home-school component, the intervention is going to fall flat. If the school is trying to intervene and the parent doesn't support the intervention, the student's behavior is not going to change. Thus a third of the ownership has to go to the parent(s) or guardian(s). A third of the ownership has to go to the school. It has to educate and follow through with positive and negative consequences. Another third of the ownership goes to the student. If the student doesn't take ownership, no behavioral plan is going to work.

An actual contract is shown in Figure 7.3. It contains replacement behaviors that, along with positive and negative consequences, are hand-tailored to the situation. The contract can't be standard because every school and parent has to have consequences that are going to fit that school and that parent, and every student has to have behaviors and consequences that are developmentally appropriate.

The home-school collaboration assumes that the troublesome behavior—even though it may be extreme—is the student's way of trying to solve an issue. What problem is he or she trying to solve? Once this is determined, it is possible to get everyone on board to help him or her solve it in a way that is not going to backfire. We capitalize on everyone's resources and strengths, including the student's. We are replacing disruptive behavior. Our focus is not on the old behavior, except to acknowledge that it has been the student's ineffective way of responding to his or her problems. We focus, instead, on the *real*, underlying problems so that we not only can solve them, but also can teach the student how to approach and cope with life problems in general.

Using the Pathways as a Common Language for Behavior

Comer emphasizes nonjudgmental descriptions of behavior that avoid imposing one's own beliefs. His metaphor of the six developmental pathways has created a framework for these descriptions and provided a way of gathering information on a wide variety of behaviors.

The most noteworthy feature of the six developmental pathways is that a common language is created among regular and special education teachers. Behavior Intervention Plans are simply not going to work in the regular classroom unless all the adults working with the students understand the plans and their underlying intentions. Special education teachers, paraprofessionals, and providers

Figure 7.3   Community School District 17 behavior management contract

Behavior Management Contract

I, _____, understand that I have a habit of

_____

Instead of this behavior, I will

_____

If I succeed, my teacher will

_____

And my parents/guardians will

_____

If I forget and do not succeed, my teacher will

_____

And my parents/guardians will

_____

Because they care about me.

Parent's signature: _____

School representative's signature: _____

Student's signature: _____

Date Signed: _____

SOURCE: Courtesy of New York City Community School District 17. Reprinted from *Six Pathways to Healthy Child Development and Academic Success: The Field Guide to Comer Schools in Action*, by James P. Comer, Edward T. Joyner, and Michael Ben-Avie. Reproduction authorized only for the local school site that has purchased this book. www.corwinpress.com.

of related services speak a language that is laden with terms from federal regulations and from the field of behavior modification. At the same time, regular education staff tend to be well versed in the language of curriculum and content areas. Often, special education staff may not be familiar with how to talk about curricular units and standardized student achievement tests. The developmental pathways are especially beneficial in these types of situations because of the "Comer mind-set" embedded within them.

One embedded aspect of the mind-set is its openness to as wide a range of options as possible, frank discussions, willingness to support the decision of the team (even when disagreeing with the decision), and a periodic reevaluation of the decision. This embedded mind-set helps to promote collegial working relationships among special and regular education staff. And collegial relationships are important to make sure that students receive the services and support that they need.

The Student as Problem Solver, Not Problem Child

Underlying this approach is an assumption that underlies all of Comer's writing and teaching, which is that the other person isn't broken: The student and the parent are doing the best they can with the resources and belief system they have at the moment, and with the experiences and role models they've had up to that point. The assumption that the student is already trying to solve the problem is a huge shift for every adult in the room and, probably, also for the student. Think of a child who up to this point has been continually put down, and now is being handed a contract to sign. Now he is seeing that the adults around him are investing themselves in him. They are saying, "We believe that you can handle one third of this important responsibility. We believe that you can make something of yourself." That's a huge shift, from being perceived as a problem child to being perceived as a problem solver on the way to successful adulthood.

PPT PROCESS CASE VIGNETTES

In case after case, after we bring the parent in and get the parent to work with us, we see the parent and the child do a complete turnaround, and we are able to resolve the problem.

In one case, what initially appeared to be a problem with one child revealed itself to be a much larger problem in family interaction:

Prior to bringing the parent in, the child had typically gone home and told his mother about whatever happened at school. The mother would say, "I'm going up to the school and beat them up" and other, similar remarks. The mother would react the same way he'd react. The mother was always blaming the school. The boy would pick this up and continue acting out.

The first parent meeting was fascinating: The mother and sister came late. The principal stormed out of the room and would not even talk to the mother. This student was a very bright little boy who had emotional problems. It appeared that the mother also had a lot of problems.

After talking to the mother, we asked the teenage sister, "Why do you think that your brother is acting out this way?" In front of the mother, the sister said, "I think it's because my mother keeps yelling at him constantly in the morning."

We turned to the mother. She explained that she was stressed in the morning because her son didn't always get dressed right away. Now we were going to help the mother solve her issues. And the sister was crying. She cried because of her own issues as well, but it changed the whole focus. The special education supervisor gave her cell phone number and her home number to the mother. And we said, "If you work with us and if you call us, then we will call you." And in this way we developed a relationship.

We have a key question about creating or improving the home-school collaboration: "If we do nothing, what do you foresee is going to happen in another few years?" The responses—including the students'—are all uncannily correct. We asked the sister, in front of her mother and brother, "What do you think is going to happen if everything stays the same? What's going to happen in a few years?" She said, "I will either be on drugs or be pregnant or I'll be dead." And the mother broke down in tears.

At that point, the mother was ready to change. She put herself in our hands, and worked with us to help solve her children's problems.

In another case, we were able to uncover the positive intention underlying a parent's unwillingness to deal with her son's misbehavior in school:

The reason why the mother had been defending her son to the hilt became clear. She was a nurse. Years ago, her husband had died in the bathroom. The mother said, "I couldn't save my husband." She felt responsible for the boy's behavior, so no matter how outrageous his behavior was in school, she kept saying, "It's not my kid, it's not my kid [who's at fault]."

Ever since then we have had a plan together. A while later, the mother came to a workshop held by one of us (Virginia Arrington). The mother wanted to speak about how she had been helped. The boy also wrote a letter to the special education supervisor in the school. He wrote: "Thank you for believing in me."

BASIC GUIDELINES FOR CHANGING BEHAVIOR

1. Avoid reacting emotionally to the misbehavior. Get into a problem-solving mode.

2. Become aware of what *triggers* the misbehavior, and change the environment to avoid these triggers.

3. Become aware of the *function* of the behavior, and provide positive ways for the student to fulfill this function (e.g., obtaining positive instead of negative attention).

4. Determine a proper replacement behavior.

5. Whenever possible, write a *contract* and have the parent, student, and administration sign it. This contract must include the positive and the negative consequences for both the old misbehavior and the new replacement behavior. These consequences must be perceived as fair by all concerned.

6. Develop a *written plan* of what staff members should do when the misbehavior is exhibited and what they should do when the proper replacement behavior is exhibited.

7. Distribute this plan to the staff so that everyone in the school knows what to do.

8. Follow through with positive and negative consequences immediately and consistently.

Inclusiveness for Children With Special Needs

Nora Martin

The Student and Staff Support Team and special educators can work together to create accommodations that enable students with special needs to study within regular classrooms.

LEAST RESTRICTIVE ENVIRONMENTS

When considering the least restrictive environment for youngsters with special needs, the developmental pathways framework is a useful guide to the accommodations and/or modifications suggested in their Individualized Education Plans (IEP). In School Development Program (SDP) schools, educators ask such questions as, "Does this lesson take into consideration the child's ability along the physical pathway?" and, "How does this lesson promote the child's ability to share (social pathway)?"

ACCOMMODATIONS FOR REGULAR CLASSROOM SETTINGS

To the maximum extent possible, the school should provide educational programs in the regular classroom setting. Accommodations that enable students qualified as in need of special services to study within regular classrooms include

- Pacing
  vary activity often
  adjust deadlines

- Environment
  reduce visual, auditory, spatial, and movement distractions
  teach positive rules for use of space

- Assignments
  provide print copy for directions given orally
  provide samples of what an "A" assignment looks like
  allow student to record or type assignment

- Presentation of Subject Matter
  preteach vocabulary
  use individual and small group instruction
  provide notes

- Motivation and Reinforcement
  plan motivated sequence of activities
  tap students' strengths and interests

- Materials
  provide typed copy of teacher material
  permit students to copy other students' notes

- Self-Management/Follow Through
  have students repeat directions
  design and use timelines for long-term assignments
  teach skills in varying settings

- Testing Adaptations
  read tests to students
  provide preview of test language
  permit oral responses

- Social Interaction Supports
  provide structured activities to create opportunities for social interaction
  teach friendship, sharing, negotiating skills
  be consistent with turn taking

The Student and Staff Support Team, in coordination with the Special Education Committee, must review on a regular basis the progress made by the children who have been qualified as in need of special services. That is how they can ensure that the school is providing the best possible educational program for this student population.

Part II

Children Need Healthy Adults

Michael Ben-Avie

To promote the balanced development of children, adults must take care of their own developmental needs. For well-functioning adults, those needs include taking care of oneself and family, personal control, respecting the rights and needs of other people, responsible citizenship, productive employment, and taking appropriate advantage of opportunities.

BALANCED DEVELOPMENT

While it seems that some children's development is balanced, we have observed that most is uneven. James P. Comer, M.D., describes children's development as growth along six interconnected pathways: physical, cognitive, psychological, language, social, and ethical. This metaphor of development is helpful in understanding how a bright child can also be socially awkward. The same child who can remember every algebraic formula might also be the one who can't remember to call his grandmother to say thank you for a gift. How is it that the bodybuilder can't manage to carry the laundry basket up the stairs? The child who has no problem telling you what you've done wrong somehow cannot seem to say, "You look tired. I'll do it."

DEVELOPMENT INTO ADULTHOOD

If children do not develop well along one of the developmental pathways, development along others may be adversely affected. It is not enough for children to be articulate if they have nothing to say. It is not enough for them to care about the community—they need experience in coordinating efforts with others.

Based on trends that we are already observing, in order to succeed most of our children will require solid knowledge in math and science as well as highly developed social knowledge of themselves and others. Our children will need to be highly flexible: apt at working on multiple projects with different teams, adaptable in their work schedule and place of employment, open in their thinking to consider the ideas of others, and willing enough to take risks. To be this flexible, they will need to be psychologically and emotionally strong. And, as the workplace becomes increasingly diverse, they will need to care about and work well with others who are not like themselves.

It is important for parents, educators, and child advocates to strive to support young people's development along all the pathways. When we do, we help to prepare them for life in an increasingly complex and challenging world. The School Development Program's (SDP) take-home message is that to promote the balanced development of young people, we have to take care of our own development. Thus Chapters 9–13 of this volume focus on adult development—our development—because adults, too, have developmental needs.

And if my back would just stop hurting ("that old physical pathway"), perhaps I could get some work done . . .

9

Teaming and Team Building

Miriam McLaughlin, Alice Huff Hart, Everol Ennis, Fred Hernández, and Jan Stocklinski

SDP depends on well-functioning teams, both to do the work of the school and to provide students with successful models of no-fault, consensus, and collaboration. The authors of this chapter are experts in teaching successful team building, teamwork, and team leadership. The fruits of their rich experience are distilled here in clear and useful guidelines, activities, and resources.

When people work together in teams, amazing things happen, particularly when members of a team share a common vision and are committed to the success of whatever they undertake. When a school district or a school recognizes the urgency of adopting a team approach, it also recognizes the need to build, restore, and strengthen functional school communities. Every team meeting becomes an opportunity to strengthen community, yet a bit more. The impetus for the adoption of a team approach to educational change is the socialization and education of the students.

Community is disrupted in meetings in which adult agendas take precedence over student-focused agendas. Community is also disrupted when teachers display an attitude of, "I'm the expert and you're not," and treat parents with disrespect. When exposed to mixed messages, children often play adults against one another and disengage from the value of schooling. On a successful school team, the teachers, the parents, the students, and the community develop and demonstrate mutual respect. Underlying a team approach is the recognition that functional school communities can be far more effective in promoting students' learning and development than can individuals working on their own.

The School Development Program (SDP) provides the structure for such success. SDP is a catalyst for positive change in school communities. The process embodied in the program empowers ordinary people to accomplish extraordinary things. Children's lives are changed as those charged with their care consider the full scope of the children's developmental needs. In SDP schools, the staff, administrators, teachers, students, and parents are partners. All engage in a problem-solving process on behalf of children. The process focuses on the strengths of all involved, especially the children. Parents, their children, and the educators who serve them experience the power of a team process that eliminates fault finding, promotes true collaboration, and engages the whole community to ensure that children have the support they need to succeed.

This chapter describes some of the features of effective team building and teaming that SDP school communities have learned over the past three decades.

EFFECTIVE TEAMS

Effective teams do not just happen: They grow to maturity. As with all development, team development can be thought of as occurring in stages, as the members get to know each other's abilities and work styles better and better. Consider a baseball team as an example. By practicing together, members of a baseball team learn which players are good at what positions. Effective teams also have roles and rules: In baseball, the coach provides leadership, helps to identify problem areas, and makes corrections to improve the team's play; there are elaborate rules for playing the game.

School teams are similarly structured. They, too, must begin meeting and working together and learning the strengths and weaknesses of team members. School teams have facilitators and administrators to help them identify problem areas and make necessary corrections so that they can plan well and make sound decisions. They also have guidelines for meeting, including time frames, a framework for appropriate discussions, and effective ways of interacting (see Figure 9.1).

Figure 9.1   To guide as we collaborate . . .

Meeting Guidelines	Dialogue Guidelines
1. Start and end on time.	1. Listen and check for understanding.
2. Take time to share personal/group successe and challenges.	2. Be succinct when conversing.
3. Adjust the agenda when necessary.	3. Value wait time.
4. Create and follow a time frame for agenda items.	4. Suspend side conversations.
	5. Speak to the entire group.

SOURCE: Courtesy of Prince George's County Public Schools, Comer Office. Reprinted from *Six Pathways to Healthy Child Development and Academic Success: The Field Guide to Comer Schools in Action*, by James P. Comer, Edward T. Joyner, and Michael Ben-Avie. Reproduction authorized only for the local school site that has purchased this book. www.corwinpress.com.

Once these structures are in place, it is up to individual team members to ensure that the team develops successfully. The success of the team does not rest solely with the administrator, facilitator, or chairperson. Each team member has a responsibility to the whole team. As with any effective team, there is good leadership and fellowship. Being on time, arriving prepared for the meeting, practicing problem solving rather than blaming, demonstrating respect for the opinions of other team members, being supportive of the work of the team, and taking responsibility for getting the work of the team accomplished are all necessary to the success of the whole team. Effective teams embrace the "we" concept and accept the fact that everyone on the team is equally responsible for helping the team reach its goal.

BUILDING RELATIONSHIPS

Without the trust and support of team members, the team cannot work together in an efficient and productive manner. Building relationships among team members is the key to building trust. Trust develops gradually as people experience their teammates' acceptance and responsiveness. As a result, members ultimately begin to feel safe with one another.

> You have to have two things at the same time—academic meetings and social meetings—because relationships need to be adjusted, and that happens only in a healthy social environment. Then you can come back to the hard discussions and really have mutual respect because everyone has had the opportunity to talk about things that are not threatening.
>
> —Fred Hernández

The process begins when team members actively and respectfully listen to one another as they share their professional and personal histories. Sharing progresses as people begin to talk about their personal goals and expectations for the team, what they hope to contribute, and what they hope to gain through their service on the team. As trust develops, team members become more willing to share ideas and opinions, they adjust their understandings of their roles and expectations of the team, and they feel increasingly valued for their contributions.

> Team members who participate in meaningful activities will quickly get to know each other. This builds social capital on the team.
>
> —Fred Hernández

We recommend that even if members know each other, start the team off at the first meeting of the year with some kind of get-acquainted or get-reacquainted activity. A retreat away from the school campus is an ideal way for people to get to know one another. If getting away is not possible, the team could set up a committee to plan a social event to take place when team members are back in school (prior to the return of the students). Structure this event so that it helps people get to know each other in somewhat personal ways.

It is critically important that each school team take an inventory of its team members. This allows the team to assess what skills members bring and how they can be best utilized in particular roles and responsibilities in order to achieve the team's shared goals. Because team dynamics can be complex, this assessment should be done each time a new team member is introduced and each time an existing member is removed or leaves.

Even when the team is working together productively, relationship building should be an ongoing process. Some teams spend a few minutes at the beginning of each meeting checking in with team members. Other teams have retreats at the beginning, in the middle, and at the end of each school year.

Finally, teams that evaluate their meetings are able to keep on top of problems members may be having relating to one another. Teams should take enough time at the close of every meeting to ask members what worked well and what needs improvement. This can bring to light issues that otherwise might compromise the effectiveness of the team's work. As long as the team exists, relationships must be renewed continually to reinforce effective and productive teamwork.

TEAMING AND TEAM BUILDING

Jan Stocklinski, former Comer director for Prince George's County Public Schools in Maryland, speaks of team development in terms of *teaming* and *team building*.

- *Teaming* refers to performing the specific actions that ensure the smooth functioning of the team. These actions include assigning roles, clarifying each other's statements, devising methods for staying on track during team discussions, taking notes, and summarizing.
- *Team building* refers to promoting relations among team members, including encouraging the quiet to speak and making sure that no one's ideas are mocked or ridiculed. Team members are encouraged to state their opinions and feelings honestly and clearly.

Both teaming and team building are essential for facilitating group problem solving. Team members learn to keep asking themselves, "What, right now, would help this group move ahead and get this problem solved?" and "What could *I* do?"

Figure 9.2 provides quality indicators of teaming and team building. Figure 9.3 offers examples of activities that give people opportunities to share. The resource list that follows can help facilitators and team members continue to build their teaming skills.

Figure 9.2　Teaming and team building

Characteristic	Beginning	Developing		Operational	Evidence of Faithful Replication
	1	2	3	4	5	

Characteristic	1	2	3	4	5	
TEAMING: Establishing and maintaining the mechanics of how to run a good meeting; actions to ensure the smooth functioning of the team						
The school community understands why teams have been established and function as they do.						
Teams are composed of representatives of the larger school community. Students participate on teams, as appropriate.						
Notice of every team meeting is well publicized.						
Teams have a written agenda for every meeting which has been developed collaboratively *well in advance* of the actual meeting.						
All team meetings have a chairperson, facilitator, timekeeper, liaison, principal/administrator, reporter, process observer, and active group members.						
Teams have a child development focus, and agendas tend to deal with improving the school's program around child development.						
Agendas usually have time allocations for each item so that there is sufficient time to discuss everyone's concerns.						
Meetings begin and end on time.						
Teams have a clearly established set of standard operating procedures that are agreed upon by all.						
Teams tend to stay on task.						
Notes are always taken during meetings and written up as minutes. Minutes are subsequently distributed to the entire school community.						
By the end of every meeting, all items have been fully discussed and members have taken responsibility for completing agreed-upon tasks.						

(Continued)

Figure 9.2 (Continued)

Characteristic	Beginning	Developing			Operational	Evidence of Faithful Replication
	1	2	3	4	5	
TEAM BUILDING: Establishing and maintaining healthy relationships among the members of a specific team (especially the degree to which members use the three guiding principles)						
Team members practice consensus.						
Team members practice collaboration.						
Team members practice no-fault.						
Team members demonstrate active listening.						
Team members appropriately express feedback to one another.						
Team members encourage quieter members to speak.						
Team members take responsibility for the quality of the interactions among members.						
Team members speak respectfully to one another.						
Team members talk about children in a descriptive, nonjudgmental manner.						
Team members support the decisions of the team, regardless of their own personal opinions.						
Team members support one another in public and when explaining team decisions to their constituent groups.						
Team members have a constructive way to bring issues and problems to the surface so that they can begin to be addressed.						
Team members actively address issues of power and control.						
Team members demonstrate that team building is an ongoing process that is never quite complete and always in need of renewal.						
Team members make sure that decisions are expressed in a clear manner that everyone in the school community will understand (i.e., no jargon).						

Team members regularly monitor and assess the progress of their team process as well as the team's effectiveness in completing tasks.						
Summary						

Figure 9.3   Activities that give people opportunities to share

---

Note: If your team has more than five or six members, split into smaller groups.

Recipes

Instruct small groups to write recipes for how they will work together during the coming year. Explain that the ingredients in the recipes will be things they believe will help the team work effectively together. For example, ingredients might include 1 cup of no-fault, a teaspoon of humor, and 1/4 cup of commitment.

Have small groups write their recipes on chart paper and post them on the wall. Invite each group to share its recipe with the whole team.

Something in the Attic

Explain that we all have mementos stored away at the back of closets or in the attic. We also have some mementos that are stored as memories just tucked away in our minds. Ask group members to dig back in their memories for a memento of their childhood and to tell their small group about it. Give a personal example to demonstrate what you expect of group members. For example, if you had a picture of you and your grandfather fishing, you could talk about the role your grandfather played in your life as a child.

Once groups have finished sharing, ask for volunteers to tell the whole group what they learned about another team member.

A Basket of Gifts

Provide each participant with a gift-wrapped box or a gift bag. Ask that they not open the boxes or bags. Explain that everyone has special gifts that help teams work more effectively together. Use yourself as an example. You might say, "I have the gift of accepting others for who they are. I believe that acceptance will help people to feel safe on our team." Be sure to gather information about the professional or technical strengths of team members.

Begin passing a large basket around the group. Instruct each participant to place their gift in the basket and share with others the gift they bring to the team.

At the end of this activity, ask the team how a variety of gifts can help the team work effectively together.

Other Activities

Other activities that build relationships may include:

- sharing plans for vacations or holidays or a special event
- sharing pictures—a great opener for people to talk about families, friends, and pets
- asking team members how they got their names, or where they were born, or what they would be doing if they were not in education
- . . . and don't forget the ultimate icebreaker—food!

TEAM BUILDING, TEAMING, AND TRAINING RESOURCES

A Compendium of Icebreakers, Energizers and Introductions
Edited by Andy Kirby
Human Resource Development Press, 1992
Amherst, MA
1-800-822-2801

Creative Training Techniques Handbook
Robert Pike
Human Resource Development
    Press, 2003
Amherst, MA
1-800-822-2801

Effective Team-Building Activities for the Sweet Potato and Pumpkin Pie Lovers
Fairy Hayes Scott and Nora Martin
Robbie Dean Press, 2003
Ann Arbor, MI
734-973-9511

Energize!
Edited by Linda Barr and Christine Harrington
Lions' Quest Program, 1991
Annapolis Junction, MD
1-800-446-2700

Even More Games Trainers Play
John W. Newstome
    and Edward E. Scannell
McGraw-Hill, 1994
New York, NY
1-800-442-9685

50 Creative Openers and Energizers
Lynn Solem and Bob Pike
Jossey-Bass/Pfeiffer, 2000
San Francisco, CA
1-877-762-2974

50 Creative Training Closers
Lynn Solem and Bob Pike
Jossey-Bass/Pfeiffer, 1998
San Francisco, CA
1-877-762-2974

50 One-Minute Tips for Trainers
Carrie A. Van Daele
Crisp Publications, 1996
Menlo Park, CA
1-800-442-7477

500 Tips for Trainers
Phil Race and Brenda Smith
Gulf Publishing, 1996
Houston, TX
713-529-4301

Instant Icebreakers
Sandy Christian (editor) and Nancy Loving
    Tubesing
Whole Person Associates, 1997
Duluth, MN
1-800-247-6789

The New Encyclopedia of Icebreakers
Miriam McLaughlin and Sandra Peyser
Jossey-Bass, 2004
San Francisco, CA
1-877-762-2974

100 Ways to Build Teams
Carol Scearce
Skylight Publishing, 1992
Pearson Skylight
Glenview, IL
1-800-348-4474

101 Ways to Make Training Active
Mel Silberman
Jossey-Bass/Pfeiffer, 2000
San Francisco, CA
1-877-762-2974

Summarizers/Activators
Jon Saphier and Mary Ann Haley
Research for Better Teaching (RBT), 1993
Acton, MA
978-263-9449

Tribes
Jeanne Gibbs
Center Source Systems, LLC, 2001
Windsor, CA
1-800-810-1701

Warm Ups and Wind Downs: 101 Activities for Moving and Motivating Groups
Sandra P. Hazouri and Miriam McLaughlin
Educational Media Corporation, 2001
Minneapolis, MN
612-781-0088

10

A Team Approach to Educational Change

J. Patrick Howley

Teams must balance their attention between the tasks they are doing and the processes by which they accomplish those tasks. To achieve this balance, SDP's director of Teaching and Adult Development presents (1) models for understanding other people, (2) concepts that support a team's sense of purpose, (3) descriptions of team members' appropriate roles, and (4) rich descriptions of specific behaviors that bring to life the guiding principles of no-fault, consensus, and collaboration.

When Connie, a fourth-grade teacher in one of our Comer schools, joined the School Planning and Management Team (SPMT), she was quite worried about whether she would be able to serve adequately as a grade-level representative. Her school had five fourth-grade teachers who were quite diverse in their approaches to teaching and learning. She didn't know what was expected of her on the team and how much she might be able to contribute. "After all," she said, "I'm just a teacher. What can I do?" In addition, she felt inadequate voicing her opinion at the meetings; there were so many people there with very strong opinions.

TWO MODELS FOR UNDERSTANDING PEOPLE'S CONCERNS

Connie's story illustrates an important point we make in the School Development Program (SDP): We must consider relationships and the personal concerns that people have as they work and interact on teams. At SDP we use two models that help us to understand these personal concerns in a general way. One is a model developed by William Schutz (1967), a psychologist and organizational consultant. Schutz says that people have three basic concerns:

1. Inclusion: Am I in or out? Do I feel included or excluded on my team?

2. Control: Do I have power to influence, or do others have more power?

3. Affection: Do I want to be close to or distant from other members of the team or school?

Another model, introduced in an affective education program directed by Gerry Weinstein (1970) at the University of Massachusetts, describes children as having three concerns:

1. Identity: Who am I?

2. Connectedness: How do I relate to others?

3. Power: Do I have any influence, power, or impact on others?

These models, which are similar and overlapping, can be viewed as personal needs of people. At any particular point in time these concerns can have a lesser or greater influence in people's lives. With or without team members' knowledge, these concerns become part of the team's dynamics. These two models can be used as a lens to understand the concerns Connie brings to the team. Connie may say to herself, "Who am I on this team?" and answer, "Well, I'm just a teacher. What can I do?" These concerns refer to identity, or may be related to power or control. If she is also wondering, "How do I relate to others?" this would be a concern with connectedness, as she thinks about her relationships with both her SPMT teammates and her colleagues in the fourth grade.

P + E + O + F + R = M: A FRAMEWORK FOR UNDERSTANDING WHY AND HOW PEOPLE SEE THE WORLD DIFFERENTLY

In our training sessions, I show a slide that says: P + E + O + F + R = M. This little formula is another way to help us understand what is happening to Connie as she comes on the team.

P + E

Connie has Perceptions (P) of both herself and others. She also has perceptions of her school, her grade level, her SPMT, and SDP. She comes to the team with previous Experiences (E). She also might experience the school as a great place to work. She might feel comfortable with her colleagues but uncomfortable with the experiences of all the changes that have taken place in the past few years.

O

She has witnessed the changes created by a new superintendent and a rapid turnover of three principals in her school. Programs have come and gone with each change of principal. These experiences influence her Organizers (O). She organizes her perceptions and experiences and creates theories to make sense of what has been happening to her. One theory might be that she believes that principals have lost touch with children by being out of the classroom so long. Therefore, the decisions the principals make may not take into account what Connie experiences with children each day in the classroom. And she might decide that the changes are too many and too soon. She might also conclude that leaders do not confer enough with teachers or include them in the decision-making process. In addition, she might determine that she is losing her touch, getting too old, and is not good enough as a teacher anymore. (This would be an identity issue in Weinstein's model, described above).

F

Feedback (F) is the verbal and nonverbal information we receive from others. Feedback might be given directly to us regarding our behavior. Sometimes we are given feedback in a deliberate, thoughtful manner. Most of the time we get feedback in a haphazard way with little thought given to how it might help or hurt us. Connie might be received as a new member of the SPMT with smiles and handshakes, or she might be ignored. She might hear immediately that members are discouraged and disheartened by all of the changes taking place, and by their inability as an SPMT to make a difference in raising test scores. She might hear that SDP focuses too much on relationships and not enough on demonstrable academic achievement. These conversations might just be gossip. They could become feedback if the team were willing to share the conversations in an open setting in which they could address the issues and, perhaps, solve the problem or the misperceptions.

R

Reflection (R) is what Connie may do as she is driving away from her first SPMT meeting. If she becomes deep in thought she may suddenly realize that she has passed her exit on the highway. During that time, she probably reflected on her perceptions of herself, the school, and the SPMT. In addition, she has reflected on her experiences in the school over the years. As she drives, she tries to make some sense of all her years in education and may even reevaluate how she thinks about the authority of the principal. She may come up with a new organizer that says, "The principal is not the only person responsible for our successes or failures. All of us are. We are in this together, and we need to collaborate. We need to make decisions by consensus. We must not continually blame each other or even our-selves, but instead live the no-fault guiding principle." These new organizers might give her new insight and new hope about what might be accomplished in her school.

M

All of the concepts described up to this point lead to creating Meaning (M). Our need is to make sense (meaning) of our perceptions, experiences, organizers, feedback, and reflections. The meaning we make can be incomplete or off the mark. We assume that the meaning we make is the *truth*. This model helps us to engage in meta-cognition—to think about our thinking. When we share our reflections with others and they share theirs with us, we are doing what we call process work. Our openness to really hearing ourselves and others will lead to a broader and more complete picture: a deeper, enriching, and more accurate meaning that is more aligned with others with whom we work.

The $P + E + O + F + R = M$ framework is part of our leadership training for two reasons. First, the framework helps participants to know that during the training they will be expected to learn in different ways. They will learn from their own perceptions and experiences in schools, from the perceptions and experiences of other participants, from the concepts presented by Yale SDP staff, from the feedback they receive, and from their own reflections during the week of the training. Experiential learning is the primary learning tool of the training. Second, participants are expected to go back to work with their colleagues who did not have these experiences. Therefore they need to create learning opportunities and experiences that replicate what they have learned in SDP's leadership training. In the training, we attend to each factor in the equation. Each perception, experience, organizer, feedback, and reflection shapes or influences how participants make meaning of their experience. This is how we learn, and this is why everyone learns differently. The school faces the challenge of each member of the school community having different perceptions, experiences, organizers, feedback they have received, and ways of reflecting. We therefore come into the school with very different ways of making meaning of the world and our school.

METHODS FOR STRENGTHENING THE WORK OF TEAMS

The Concept of the Container

The equation described above highlights differences in concerns, needs, viewpoints, energy, focus, and interests. Given the diversity and complexity of human beings, it might seem almost impossible to bring even a small group of individuals to a common understanding, much less to a commitment to action. All of these differences can be described as energy. It is easy to imagine all of this energy going in all different directions. The question becomes, "How can we contain, support, and focus all of this energy so that the energy is aligned, complementary, and integrated into common causes?"

The leadership training introduces the concept of the container after participants have discussed the many concerns they have about relationships in their schools. The container seen in Figure 10.1 shows the children we work with placed inside a figurative container of adult hands. This concept of a container holding and supporting a group of children, or a plan or a concept, can be a powerful model for helping a group of people to guide their common work. No one can go it alone anymore. We need one another in order to fulfill our responsibilities to our schools and children. The concept of the container provides an opportunity for participants to reflect on how they can respond more effectively to the diversity of needs, feelings, and thinking of team members. Knowledge of the concept of the container helps us take the energy of a team, whether positive or negative, and channel it productively into focusing on problem solving for the developmental needs of children.

Figure 10.1 Providing consistent expectations and support for children

Imagine me standing before you with a container, a paper bag. I take a pitcher of water and pour the water into it. The water almost immediately begins to spill out. Just as water spills out of the container, so do children act out and misbehave. If the container is not strong enough, it cannot support their healthy development. I use this illustration of the container to make three points.

Point One: Family, School, and Places of Worship

First, focusing on the child, I ask, "What are the containers that both support and contain children in our society?" The typical answers are family, school, and places of worship. The consistent messages of these three structures and our expectations of children's behavior give children the containers they need for their healthy development. As adults work together on what is best for children and their development, they are building a strong container.

It is the communication among the adults in these structures (family, school, places of worship) that prevents children from "falling through the cracks." An example of communication between the school and the community comes from a principal in one of our districts who visited a nearby store where children from her school hung out. In talking with the store owner, she learned that many children were eating junk food, and some children were stealing items from the store. This was exactly the type of communication she desired with store owners in the school's neighborhood.

At another time, she visited a condominium near the school because she had heard that children were going in and going out of one of the residences during the school day. She next met with the police so they could patrol both the store and the condominium and look into the activities of the students in their neighborhood. She also met with parents and brought the concerns to their attention. As the parents, teachers, principal, police, condominium management association, and store owner work together, they are creating a strong container. The children will experience adults working together to ensure they act in appropriate ways. The need for and the power of the container is obvious in this context.

Point Two: The Guiding Principles: Consensus, Collaboration, No-fault

Second, I make the point that the three guiding principles should act as the container for all the teams: the School Planning and Management Team (SPMT) and any committee that the SPMT sets up, the Student and Staff Support Team (SSST), and the Parent Team (PT). As members commit themselves to using the guiding principles, their actions on the teams are led not by finding fault with others or blaming people, but instead by working toward addressing and trying to solve problems.

A commitment to collaborative relationships enables team members to hear one another and to support one another by building on the comments in the dialogue. Dialogue does not mean thinking alike. As described by David Bohm (1992), it is "thinking together" (p. 204). A commitment to consensus enables us to make higher quality decisions. In order for the three guiding principles to work, we first have to agree that these are our expectations, agreements, and commitments to our team. This makes a strong container for the teams (see Figure 10.2).

Figure 10.2 Providing consistent expectations and support for parents and staff

Point Three: The Principal and the Teams

Third, I make the point that the SPMT itself and the other members of the school community also need to have a container. The principal, chairperson, and facilitator form a container by meeting on a regular basis to discuss the work of the SPMT. They should look at SDP documents that describe effective teams and ask each other questions such as: "Are we process oriented?" "Does the team have a sense of community?" "Is there trust?" "Do we have effective relationships on the teams so that people are working together and accomplishing their tasks?" They also need to ask: "Are we task oriented?" "Are we focusing on our Comprehensive School Plan at our meetings?" "Do we focus on solving problems?" "Are we using our time effectively?" "What can each of us do to attend to both task and relationship issues?"

When the leaders in the school meet on a regular basis, they are forming a psychological container. While in this container, the leaders discuss emotionally charged issues relevant to the school community so that all of the energy in the school is being guided in a positive direction for children. What I have described is a container, within a container, within a container. This ensures that—like a strong paper cup, within a strong paper cup, within a strong paper cup—no water can possibly spill out, no child will fall through the cracks, no child will drop out of the psychological containers that we have created.

What helps Connie, and indeed all members of the school community, is knowing that their concerns about children will be heard and addressed. Everyone needs to know that each one has a responsibility to participate in improving the school. Connie needs to know that she has a role to play on the team. The descriptions found below help all to know the work of the SPMT and the responsibilities of its members.

Activation of Team Roles

Activation of team roles is another method for strengthening the work of teams. Because people are different, their perceptions of the world and the school differ. And because people become team members with many different and personal concerns, the challenge for the team is to perceive the diversity as a strength instead of a liability. When an SPMT uses the guiding principles of no-fault, collaboration, and consensus, they strengthen their work as a team. These principles help build a strong container for supporting what is inside. These roles help the team to see that everyone is responsible for making the team and the school work efficiently and effectively. The roles are described below.

Group Member (applicable to all team members)

On collaborative teams all members are very *active*. The members control what happens during meetings. Members contribute their ideas, insights, opinions, and suggestions, and they give feedback about both the tasks (the content of the meetings) and the process (how the team works together). Each member's *voice* on the team is important and should be heard. Many members of the team have dual roles (see below). As a team evolves, the need diminishes for formally designating who fulfills which role because all members of the team will take responsibility for the following:

- telling the people whom they represent about the team's accomplishments
- helping the team to stay on task
- listening and helping all members to be heard
- looking at the school from a global perspective and helping make decisions that are best for children and the entire school community
- asking continuously for input; sharing thoughts, feelings, and perceptions; and asking for feedback

- setting the agenda in accordance with feedback received from constituent groups
- collecting and analyzing data to help make decisions regarding teaching, learning, and the curriculum
- taking notes and clarifying communication both within the team, and between the team members and the rest of the school population

Chairperson

The chairperson has a key role—and one of the most difficult roles—on a team. The chairperson helps the team create agendas and the time frame for each item on the agenda. During the meeting, the chairperson keeps the team on task, guiding the team by keeping it focused on addressing the items on the agenda and accomplishing tasks within the time frames. The chairperson should meet with the principal and facilitator both before and after meetings to discuss how to help the meetings run effectively. The chairperson orchestrates the meeting, looking often to the principal and facilitator to ensure that tasks address issues from a schoolwide perspective, and that attention is paid to details. The chairperson also looks to see if the work of the team is balanced between task work and process work. The chairperson guides the team through the agenda as quickly and smoothly as possible, and yet slowly enough that members of the team can fully address all of the relevant issues.

Principal/Administrator

The administrator helps set up meeting times and locations, and ensures that the notes of the meetings are distributed to everyone in the school community. The presence of a school administrator at all meetings helps members to recognize the importance of the work of the team. Rather than running the meeting, the administrator supports the work of the chairperson and facilitator. The administrator guides from a distance by having meetings with the chairperson and facilitator before and after the team meeting. During the meeting the administrator helps members see the big picture of the school, the school community, board issues, and city, state, and federal issues. In addition, the administrator helps to define or clarify the parameters of the team's power, as well as district issues that impact on the principal and, as a result, the team. The principal also informs the team of the superintendent's decisions, budget constraints, board policy, school law, and state mandates.

Facilitator

The facilitator has the most difficult role. The facilitator listens simultaneously to the content of the discussion and the process: Who talks and for how long? Who is not so active? When there are differences or conflicts, has each side of a conflict been heard completely? At the same time, the facilitator listens to the content of the meeting in order to contribute as a member and to be able to know if the content is on or off track. The facilitator must work with the chairperson and principal during, before, and after meetings. On larger teams or teams with many diverse and strong differences, it may be helpful to have two facilitators. The facilitator makes interventions to help clarify issues, help people listen to one another, help everyone participate, and help clarify communication among people on the team if there are misunderstandings. The facilitator watches to see how to help the chairperson run the meeting, and to see if people are on board with both the content and the process. If people have come late or have to leave for a while, the facilitator ensures that they have the information and support to be effective team members.

If the team gets stuck in any way, the facilitator helps the team get unstuck and accomplish what it has set out to do. The facilitator does this primarily by stopping or slowing down the task work and asking questions about the process. The facilitator also watches for confusion, invites people to ask questions, and tries to help the team process in any way, such as shutting the door if there is too much outside noise or getting paper and pencils for people who forgot to bring their own. The facilitator is the caretaker of the whole team process.

Notetaker (Recorder)

If detailed minutes need to be recorded, two people should be responsible for this role, both so that the notes will be complete, and so that each notetaker will also have the time to be an active team member. Rather than recording everything that is discussed, often just the key issues, decisions, and rationale for the decisions are needed for the record. The level of detail should be decided by the team as one of the mutually agreed upon rules. At the end of each meeting, the notetaker(s) should review the minutes with the team.

Timekeeper

Periodically during the meeting, the timekeeper lets members know how much time has been allotted for an agenda item and how much time still remains for that agenda item. The team can renegotiate their time frames as needed. Some timekeepers make cards that say "15 minutes remaining," "10 minutes remaining," and "5 minutes remaining." They hold them up as reminders.

Liaison

The liaison represents the team by reporting its progress to other teams. The liaison might create a newsletter to help inform those outside the team or community. The liaison also collects information from other teams and passes it on to team members. The liaison could also meet with other liaisons to discuss similar agenda items and process issues (e.g., how to improve meetings). This information is then shared with team members.

Reporter

The reporter is the spokesperson for the team, representing the voices of the team and ensuring that communication and collaboration occur among teams. In large trainings or large meetings, the reporter's role is to report out to the larger community of participants a summary of the team discussion.

Process Observer

In the past, the process observer in our Leadership Training 102 has not been a member of the team. At the same time that the team members have been engaged in learning and interacting on their team, the process observer has been trained to observe and take notes about what is said and done by team members. The primary role of the process observer is to help the team learn about team processes and group dynamics. The process observer does this by providing nonjudgmental feedback to the team near the end of each day of training. Because in a collaborative team everyone is expected to be a leader in some way, the focus of the feedback is on the leadership behavior of the team members. The framework for the feedback also relates to the three guiding principles; the six developmental pathways; the gifts, strengths, and contributions of members; and how the team can improve its effectiveness.

ROLE EXPECTATION CARDS

Cards have been created to give team members visual reminders of the expectations of their own role and the roles of others. The group member card is a reminder for all members of the team to always be actively engaged, either by listening, speaking, leading, or following. This card sits in the middle of the table to remind all members to be active participants. The cards help those new to the team or those observing to see that the team has a protocol that guides their work together. Figure 10.3 shows the expectations listed on the role cards that are placed on the tables at all meetings to remind members of how they can work together more effectively.

Figure 10.3 Role expectation cards

Group Member (applicable to all members of the team)
- Represent voices of the school community
- Communicate back to the school community or group represented the decisions made by the team
- Communicate the reasons for those decisions
- Be very active on the team and contribute ideas, insights, opinions, and suggestions
- Listen, listen, and listen some more!
- Be willing to support a team decision, even if you do not fully agree with it

Chairperson
- Help create an agenda with input from team members
- Call the meeting to order
- Define the tasks clearly
- Keep the team on task
- Expedite the making of decisions
- Keep discussions focused on children and the agenda items

(Continued)

Figure 10.3 (Continued)

Principal/Administrator

- Help set up meeting locations and times
- Ensure that information is distributed as needed
- Help members see the "big picture" (school board issues, goals, state and district mandates, etc.)
- Help define and clarify parameters of the team's power and responsibility
- Help identify issues that might relate to the principal, superintendent, budget, board policy, school law, etc
- Help make the meetings child centered

Facilitator

- Support the chairperson and the principal by helping the team with its process (relationship) issues
- Listen actively
- Help everyone participate
- Help everyone to be heard
- Clarify confusion or differences by paraphrasing what is heard
- Help differences to be discussed and resolved
- Support and ensure that information summarized by the reporter or notetaker is communicated to other groups and teams

Notetaker (Recorder)

- Record minutes of the meeting
- List the key decisions made by the team
- Record who will do what and when
- Provide copies of minutes for the entire school community
- Maintain a file of the minutes for each meeting

Timekeeper

- Let the team members know when they are at midpoint in time on an agenda item
- Let the team know when five minutes are left and when one minute is left
- Negotiate for more time if it is needed
- Help the team begin and end on time, or negotiate to change time frame

Reporter

- Discuss with the team the notes taken by the notetaker
- Decide with the team the most important or relevant information to report out
- Summarize the information and any key decisions made that other groups might need to know
- Stand up and deliver the information to the larger group (e.g., at a training event)

Process Observer

- Take notes on behaviors seen that help or hinder the tasks and relationships
- Provide nonjudgmental feedback about observed behaviors at the end of the meeting or the beginning of the next meeting
- Help the team have a dialogue on its effectiveness (may sometimes be done in conjunction with the facilitator)

FEEDBACK DESCRIPTION GUIDES

The Feedback Description Guides that appear in Figures 10.4, 10.5, and 10.6 are also useful tools for strengthening the work of teams. The behavior descriptions listed in each guide help to further clarify which behaviors help or hinder the team.

Figure 10.4 Feedback description guide: Consensus

Task behaviors are behaviors that help the team to accomplish its tasks.	
Using this task behavior . . .	**. . . the team member or team . . .**
Initiating	helps define what tasks need to be done; suggests goals or action steps.
Seeking information	asks questions seeking opinions, perceptions, and data from team members, the larger school community, and others.
Informing	offers facts, gives opinions, presents needed information to the team.
Clarifying	repeats or interprets what has been said or decided and asks for confirmation.
Summarizing	synthesizes what has been discussed and draws a conclusion for the team to consider.
Testing reality	checks to see if an idea or information fits with the data. Checks to see if an idea or suggestion will work.
Directing	helps the team create and maintain a sense of direction.
Pressing for results	keeps the team on task to accomplish its goals.
Systematizing	offers suggestions for organizing data with procedures (e.g., charts); provides procedures or strategies for accomplishing tasks.
Making decisions	helps the team make decisions through data gathering, prodding the team, offering procedures and options for next steps.

SOURCE: Adapted in part from the work of NTL/Learning Resources Corporation (1976) in their publication, "Role Functions in a Group." Reprinted from *Six Pathways to Healthy Child Development and Academic Success: The Field Guide to Comer Schools in Action*, by James P. Comer, Edward T. Joyner, and Michael Ben-Avie. Reproduction authorized only for the local school site that has purchased this book www.corwinpress.com.

Figure 10.5 Feedback description guide: Collaboration

Process or maintenance behaviors are behaviors that build and maintain the teams' working relationships.	
Using this process or maintenance behavior . . .	**. . . the team member or team . . .**
Showing care and warmth	shows concern and respect for the viewpoints of others. Seeks to include others.
Demonstrating listening	paraphrases other people's comments.
Giving feedback	describes the specific behavior and describes how it affects others on the team.
Asking for feedback	seeks input from the team (example: "Is this working?" "Am I off track here?" "What is the best way for us to proceed?").
Being open, and "leveling"	says what they feel, what they are concerned about or appreciate, and what they want or need.
Showing empathy	demonstrates understanding of how the other person experiences things.
Staying in the present	is in tune with what is happening on this team, now, rather than discussing "How we used to do it" or getting impatient and wanting to get on to the next step.
Harmonizing	attempts to help people explore differences and reconcile disagreements.
Gate keeping	suggests procedures that facilitate participation. Suggests ways for people to communicate more openly.
Exploring differences	helps the team look at another point of view by asking if someone might see a situation differently.
Testing consensus	asks team for agreement on an issue to see if the team is ready for a decision.
Encouraging	acknowledges and promotes the contributions of others.
Compromising	admits to own errors and willingly compromises.
Facilitating conflicts	wants to hear both sides of a disagreement; asks each person or a representative of each side of an argument to discuss further what they feel and why they feel that way.
Setting standards	helps clarify what the team is trying to do or to accomplish.

SOURCE: Adapted in part from the work of NTL/Learning Resources Corporation (1976) in their publication, "Role Functions in a Group." Reprinted from *Six Pathways to Healthy Child Development and Academic Success: The Field Guide to Comer Schools in Action*, by James P. Comer, Edward T. Joyner, and Michael Ben-Avie. Reproduction authorized only for the local school site that has purchased this book. www.corwinpress.com.

Figure 10.6 Feedback description guide: No-fault

Nonfunctional behaviors are behaviors that do not contribute to either the group's task or process. Functional behaviors support both task and process.		
When this unproductive behavior arises . . .	**Use this functional behavior . . .**	**. . . so that the team member or team . . .**
Blaming	Focusing on solving problems (No blaming)	does not find fault with staff, parents, the team, or other teams. Instead, individuals try to solve problems by sharing ideas and offering strategies.
Aggression	Respecting others (Lack of aggression)	does not attack individuals or groups (including joking about them). Instead, gives nonjudgmental feedback.
Fighting	Attending to process (No fighting)	does not argue by going over the same ground again and again. Instead, will compromise or offer alternative ideas.
Controlling	Recognizing others' rights (Refraining from controlling)	does not control the meetings by talking over others, interrupting, or attempting to get others to agree with them. Instead, encourages others to share their points of view.
Drifting	Staying on task (Absence of drifting)	does not go off on tangents that are not relevant to the team task or process. Instead, remains focused and on task at all times.
Blocking	Remaining flexible (No blocking)	does not block the team by disagreeing beyond reason, stubbornly resisting, or having and/or pursuing a hidden agenda. Instead, is open and willing to consider new ideas.
Dominating	Sharing time and power (No dominating)	does not dominate the meetings or monopolize the time or the topics being discussed by the team. Instead, encourages others to participate.
Out-of-field	Putting the team's needs first (No out-of-field behavior)	does not display out-of-field behaviors such as not being on task, seeking attention or recognition. Instead, notices what the team needs from its members and provides help when needed or asked for.
Avoidance	Tolerating conflict (No avoidance)	does not engage in such avoidance behavior as changing the subject or the use of humor to avoid conflict. Instead, listens to the conflicts and may use humor to help members feel more at ease to talk more openly.
Withdrawing	Being fully present (No withdrawing)	does not withdraw physically or emotionally, leaving the team and not actively participating. Instead, eyes, body, and comments always demonstrate full attention to the tasks and concerns of the team.
Sarcasm	Being courteous (No sarcasm)	does not make cutting or hurtful comments with the intent of shaming or ridiculing. Instead, says kind words that help members to feel a part of the team.
Ignoring	Being inclusive (No ignoring)	does not disregard the statements of another person. Instead, acknowledges any comments made by the members of the team.

SOURCE: Adapted in part from the work of NTL/Learning Resources Corporation (1976) in their publication, "Role Functions in a Group." Reprinted from *Six Pathways to Healthy Child Development and Academic Success: The Field Guide to Comer Schools in Action*, by James P. Comer, Edward T. Joyner, and Michael Ben-Avie. Reproduction authorized only for the local school site that has purchased this book. www.corwinpress.com.

The information in the feedback guides enables team members to have a common language (language pathway) for giving no-fault feedback. In addition, the guides help members address process issues and still remain respectful (ethical pathway) of one another. By using these guides to talk about their own processes, team members improve their work and strengthen their relationships with one another (social pathway). The process observer and, eventually, all team members can use these guides to help reflect and assess (process), give feedback on what is working or not working on their team, and then make specific changes to improve their work.

REFERENCES

Bohm, D. (1992). *Thought as a system*. London: Routledge.

NTL/Learning Resources Corporation. (1976). Role functions in a group. In J. W. Pfeiffer & J. E. Jones (Eds.), *The 1976 annual handbook for group facilitators*. La Jolla, CA: University Associates.

Schutz, W. (1967). *Joy*. New York: Grove Press.

Weinstein, G. (1970). *Toward humanistic education: A curriculum of affect*. New York: Praeger.

READ MORE ABOUT . . .

For information on how the well-functioning of teams depends on an understanding of people's differences, see Chapter 12 in this volume, "It's All About Effective Relationships: Frameworks for Understanding Ourselves and Others."

For information about feedback, see the discussion of the Jo-hari Window in Chapter 12 in this volume, "It's All About Effective Relationships: Frameworks for Understanding Ourselves and Others."

11

Establishing a Foundation

A Principal's View of Task and Process

Jeffery German with J. Patrick Howley and Michael Ben-Avie

In a report from the field, a former middle school principal tells the story of how his school discovered, familiarized itself with, and finally embraced the Comer Process, learning along the way to trust the processes that support the tasks. The reflections section that follows discusses important lessons contained in the story.

HOW OUR SCHOOL USED TO BE

When I became principal of Welborn Middle School (Guilford County, North Carolina) in 1995, we had 531 students. About 56 percent of our students received free or reduced-price lunch. There had been three principals during the previous four years. The teacher turnover rate was pretty high. Behavioral expectations had not been communicated to the students in a way that they accepted. Fighting was quite common in the hallways and in the cafeteria. Many of the parents and teachers were frustrated that students were undisciplined and were not willing participants in the teaching and learning process.

The outward appearance of the school was not inviting because a fence surrounded it. I never learned whether this was designed to discourage break-ins or to project a safe environment, but it did neither. We discussed the fence with the staff and parents, and we made a decision to remove it. We felt that it didn't send the right message to the community. Schools should be perceived as being community oriented, community based, and inviting to everyone who enters the front doors.

One of the next things we did was to introduce the School Development Program (SDP) to the school community. Although I had heard about it for years, my first true exposure to SDP and my subsequent training took place while I was assistant principal at the high school next door. Achievement outcomes at Welborn were not very high when I arrived. We scored in the middle 50th to low 60th percentile in reading. In math, we scored between the 61st and 62nd percentiles. After we introduced the Comer Process, the students' test scores increased as they moved from one grade level to the next. By the third year of our implementation of the Comer Process, our school had been promoted by the state from "Adequate Performance" status to "Exemplary" based on the percentage of students on grade level in math, reading, and writing. Students returned to Welborn from private schools and from other schools outside their assigned district. With this increase in the size of the student body, we were able to gain an additional assistant principal, bringing the total to two. We felt that we were getting students back because parents felt good about the Comer Process. (Eventually we got up to almost 900 students, but that was due in large part to the district's lines being redrawn in 2001.)

At the end of my first year, the PTA actually had me honored by the entire school system's PTA council. Many visitors came in to take a look at how we were implementing SDP; a group of educators came from as far away as Detroit, Michigan, to see how we ran our School Planning and Management Team (SPMT) meeting. We were also fortunate that the school system selected us to be observed by the Rockefeller Foundation's research team from the University of North Carolina. They looked at SDP's impact on the changes that had taken place at the school. They interviewed administrators, parents, staff, business partners, employees, and students. Based on the findings of the research team, Welborn was selected as one of five schools in the United States to be identified as an exemplary Comer school. I also received SDP's Patrick Francis Daly Memorial Award for Excellence in Educational Leadership, which made me very pleased for the school, staff, student body, and community. In my last two years as the principal at Welborn Middle School (2001–2002 and 2002–2003), we were named one of the 15 most improved schools out of the 105 schools in our system.

INTRODUCING THE COMER PROCESS TO THE STAFF

When I became principal, one of the first things I wanted to do was to meet with the school's leadership team and start the process of assessing the school. Together, we listed the issues and the problems they had been dealing with over the past few years. The number one concern for the leadership team was discipline. Other concerns included curriculum issues, parental apathy, student activities, attendance, public relations, human relations, climate, discipline, and staff development. After the concerns were identified, I said to the leadership team, "How do you propose that we go about addressing these? What have you done in the past? What do you anticipate that we can do in the future to address these?" We brainstormed.

I informed the leadership team that I knew of a program that I wanted to share with them. I gave them a brief overview of the Comer Process. I cautioned them that it was just my opinion that this program could address some of these concerns, and that they didn't have to accept it. I assessed how they felt about it. I said, "If you think we should pursue it, then we will go forward. The next thing we would do is to share it with the entire staff. If they feel that we should go forward, then we'll do that." I stressed, "If at any point someone feels that they have another program that will help us address our concerns, I have no problem with that. I'm just sharing with you what I feel works."

I introduced the nine elements of the Comer Process and made sure that relationships and trust were emphasized. Those two areas had to be focused on because by looking at data I discovered that some of the staff members didn't really feel good about each other. The principal before me had developed a questionnaire: "What grade level would you like to work on next year?" "What team would you like to be assigned to?" What I found interesting on the surveys was that people stated that they didn't want to work with a certain person, and why. I got a sense that we had to deal with some relationship issues. The working relationships and the environment were not conducive to getting the kinds of results we should have been getting. I proposed the Comer Process to the leadership team, and they bought into it. We presented it to the faculty, and they bought into it. The next step was to share with the staff a means for addressing the concerns they had identified. Sharing the subcommittee structure with them, I explained that the subcommittees would be forums for dealing with each of the concerns they had identified, and would be an extension of the SPMT. I developed a brief description of what participation in each one of the subcommittees would entail, and had them sign up for the subcommittee of their choice. The Comer Process at Welborn Middle School was born at that point. We put a process in place through which we were saying to people, "Okay. You've identified the problems, and here is the format that we will use to arrive at the solutions."

INTRODUCING THE SIX DEVELOPMENTAL PATHWAYS

Our next challenge was to identify how understanding the six developmental pathways might become the link that would allow us to help students become more successful in the classroom. We spent a great deal of time on the pathways, sharing them with staff, students, and parents. It was important to get teachers to understand that the notion of relationships transcends how well you get along with the teacher next door; it also includes how well you get along with the students and parents. When we talked about the linkage between relationships and the pathways, we had to help teachers understand how this linkage could offset some of the students' behavior and nonparticipation problems.

For example, we were able to say, "Be careful how you interact with students. Don't be sarcastic with them. One of the things you need to recognize is that when you are sarcastic, tease, and play with students, they may not be ready to bring it to an end when you are. If they're not ready, and you make the decision to punish them, there are ethical pathway issues that you need to look at within yourself." We played out as many scenarios as possible to help teachers experience that they first had to look within themselves to get a better understanding of what the pathways meant for them. This introspection would enable them to recognize the characteristics and traits that students bring into the classroom, and what we could do to help students grow and develop along each pathway.

One example I used with teachers was this: "What happens when you realize that you've had a tough time trying to motivate and stimulate some of the students in your class, and you want to try something new? You go home and develop a lesson plan that you get really excited about because you know that it will keep Johnny involved and sitting on the edge of his seat. This is *the* lesson plan! But, when you drive to work the next morning, you get pulled over for speeding, and you get a ticket. Now you are thinking of insurance points and increased premiums. So the level of excitement you felt when you left home has changed tremendously by the time you get to school. You now have a psychological pathway issue that you have to put in order before you meet your students. If you can't straighten out that pathway issue within yourself, you're not going to motivate and stimulate your students. The same holds true for Johnny. If Johnny is sitting in your classroom and he is lethargic and he has his head on his desk or he's looking around and not participating, the first thing we need to do is find out what the problem is. I know that when Johnny is up and involved he has created some challenges for us, but we still have a responsibility to make sure that he gets a proper education."

INTRODUCING THE TEAMS

We started talking about the various teams that we have in place, such as the Student and Staff Support Team (SSST), which may be the outlet to use if you can't reach Johnny on your own by interacting with him and his parents. If the various referrals that you have made to the counselor, the administration, and others haven't proven to be successful, the next step would be to make sure that he is referred to the SSST. The group of assembled professionals who look at some of Johnny's unique challenges usually provides some options not available in the classroom. As we talked about the teams, we realized that we needed to promote our own development in behalf of the students.

To introduce the value of exploring our own development along the six pathways, I reported an anecdote about myself: One of the things I shared with the teachers is that prior to becoming principal at Welborn I was principal at another school in another system. At that school, very selfishly, I had fought the whole notion of providing breakfast for students because I was looking at it from the standpoint of having to provide supervision: "It becomes another one of those things I have to be responsible for." As I became part of the Comer Process and started understanding the pathways, I had to go back and look at myself from an ethical perspective. I realized that I had been responsible for affecting my students' physical pathways in a negative manner.

When I first got to Welborn we didn't have the breakfast program. But then the funding became available and we were targeted as one of the schools that would be offering breakfast. Some of the teachers were reluctant, so I shared that anecdote with them to let them know that we must look within ourselves and begin to realize that we have to focus on our pathways so we don't infringe upon pathways of others. We've got to make sure these kids eat breakfast because if they don't eat breakfast, they are not going to grow and develop well, and they are not going to go into the classroom and perform to the extent that we'd like them to.

Incorporating the three teams into our organizational format was challenging for some teachers because of the adjustments they had to make. We needed to make sure that everybody at the school would be afforded an opportunity at some time to be a part of the leadership team. That didn't go over well with some folks; we heard that some of them had been part of this team for 10 or 15 years and felt that they had done some good things. We heard other people say, "Well, you know, what you have to recognize is that, generally, the people on the leadership team are the ones who will step to the plate if you need something done, and they'll make sure it's done." I agreed with them, but I said, "We have to change that. We've got to make sure that everybody understands that it becomes his or her responsibility to help out. We have a subcommittee structure in place here now, and everybody is going to take an active role in it." So, on every team, we made sure that we constantly talked about the importance of trust, establishing relationships, and making sure that when we interact with each other, each of us has got to give in a little bit. We said, "If what you've been holding onto is not in the best interests of children, you need to find an alternative solution."

INTRODUCING THE GUIDING PRINCIPLES

We stressed the guiding principles: "We can't be successful on any one of these teams until each person makes an effort to collaborate." We also stressed the importance of making decisions through consensus. Defining the difference between arriving at decisions through voting versus the input/feedback process of the consensus decision-making principle was challenging, at times, for me as well as for the staff. But, consensus decision making provides everyone an opportunity to participate in arriving at the final decision. Whether you like the final decision or not is a whole different issue.

I have a story to tell about that. Introducing the no-fault principle wasn't easy because blaming others had been a way of life for too long. Still, we needed to make sure that student learning and development was our major focus. We needed to make sure that the number of disciplinary referrals was reduced. When I shared data, I didn't say, "Mr. Johnson sends more kids to the office than anybody else," or "Certain teachers are not performing as well as they should." Instead, we shared the results of data from tests and surveys, and we discussed problems. Next, we tried to identify some solutions. We were not pointing fingers. We were not blaming. We were simply saying, "We have some work to do."

People had the most difficulty with the principle of no-fault. It had been convenient for people to pass blame along to others. I wouldn't say they were doing it in a malicious manner. I think they wanted to make sure that somebody understood that they were doing their job, and couldn't do it better because the people before them didn't do their job. We heard from the sixth-grade teachers, "If the fifth-grade teachers had done a better job of teaching math, then we would get better results from our students." I think we can take the blame game all the way back to conception and talk about the genes of our students. What we must focus on, however, is where students are on the learning curve when we get them, and we have to go forward from there. We've got to find out where students' deficiencies are, and then address the deficiencies individually. We kill more time discussing why we're not having the degree of success we should have, or why the kids are not having the degree of success they should have, rather than recognizing that we've got to work with students based on their individual ability.

MAINTAINING THE GUIDING PRINCIPLES WHILE THINKING STRATEGICALLY: "WE DON'T VOTE"

We tried to identify strategies that we could use to increase student learning, particularly for the students who had been identified as performing below grade level. Tutoring became a major area that we wanted to discuss further. One of the leadership team members said that we could provide tutoring for the students first thing in the morning. We discussed the logistics: So many of our students ride the bus, and by the time they get here it's time for breakfast, and there isn't time to tutor them. Another suggestion was to provide tutoring for students after school. I said jokingly, "If you don't rope them and make sure that you keep them here, they're going to get on the bus and go home." I also reminded the team that a lot of students experienced some degree of success in school because of their involvement in extracurricular activities, and we wanted to support that success.

I asked the leadership team how they would feel about the possibility of taking these students out of their elective classes a couple of times a week. We discussed the logistics of doing that, and they bought into it. We included it as an agenda item for our faculty meeting the next day. Any decision made by the leadership team is discussed with the entire staff, and any schoolwide issue is decided through consensus. I designed the agenda for the meeting with that item as one of the last items because the other items wouldn't take long, and I thought the meeting was going to be brief. We moved rapidly through the agenda, and when I got to that item I said, "I'm really excited about the proposal that's come out of the leadership team because I think we have developed a process that will help our Level I and Level II students." I explained that the new tutoring process would involve taking these students out of different elective classes twice a week. "They'll come out of one class on Tuesday, and a different class on Thursday." After that explanation, I was waiting for everybody to give his or her approval so we could wrap up the meeting.

An elective teacher raised her hand and said, "If you take a student out of my class, he's going to get farther behind." We listened to others, and I was thinking, "The reason why we're taking the children out is because they are already behind and we're trying to see what we can do to bring them all up to speed." The discussion went back and forth for about 45 minutes. We continued to debate how this was going to impact the elective teachers. I actually reached a point where I said, "Let's vote." And one of the teachers stood up and said, "Mr. German, we don't vote."

> I actually reached a point where I said, "Let's vote." And one of the teachers stood up and said, "Mr. German, we don't vote."

That was great to hear. We talked for another 10 or 15 minutes, and I reminded them about consensus and the process of having input, and the willingness to buy into a decision. I also reminded them of the assessment and modification component of the Comer Process that allowed us to reflect periodically on our decisions and adjust them if needed. I said, "If it's not working, we'll come back and make necessary adjustments." We approved the tutoring plan and adjourned with a better understanding of how consensus worked. That's how we have addressed our major decisions ever since.

REFLECTIONS ON THE "WE DON'T VOTE" STORY: A CONVERSATION ABOUT RELATIONSHIPS, TEAMS, MEETINGS, AND TRUST

I had the opportunity to talk about the "We Don't Vote" faculty meeting with Pat Howley and Michael Ben-Avie from the New Haven office of the SDP. Excerpts from our taped conversation follow.

MICHAEL BEN-AVIE: Jeff's story about wanting to vote captures the mood I'm in a lot of the time at SDP. I am very task oriented. And the truth of the matter is, that I can barely stand attending some of these SDP meetings. Sometimes I stir up trouble just to entertain myself. I recognize the feeling Jeff had when he said, "Let's vote"—let's get it over with and go home! So I want to ask you about that, Pat. How would you respond to that? What happened at that meeting? What happened when he reached that frustration point?

PAT HOWLEY: He's responsible for making sure that they get something accomplished. You have a person who is more task oriented, at least at that moment, and then you have people who had some process issues, relationship issues, internal and interpersonal conflicts and differences. One issue can open up a can of worms, and then a lot of issues get thrown into the mix. And then it feels like chaos, particularly to the person who is ultimately responsible for a final decision, and also, has to answer to someone else. It feels like, "This is total disintegration." I also feel that sometimes.

We have validated that people have feelings. Just as you were frustrated, other people might be frustrated about whatever can of worms we opened up. Their levels of frustration have been building over the years. So it erupts, given either the climate we've created, or the process we're following. I have just come back from a training at which someone said during the process time, "Well, I felt overwhelmed because I felt like you dumped two roles on me:

reporter and recorder. And you really didn't give me any chance to respond to that. I was uncomfortable all morning having two roles—roles that I didn't really have the opportunity to choose. It was thrust on me." In a school it might be thrust on them by the principal, and it may be thrust on the principal by central office.

JEFFERY GERMAN: What heightened my level of frustration was that I was trying to share a process with them and they were not buying into it. What was so encouraging was the teacher's reminding me that we don't vote. This is what the process is all about. There are going to be some levels of frustration. We were talking about trying to reach something through consensus. And I was referring back to what creates all kinds of discord for us, the "let's vote" mentality. And somebody said, in effect, "Well, that's unacceptable." That's when I felt like we were trying to become a Comer school. When somebody other than the principal could step up and say, "We don't do it that way."

PAT HOWLEY: Now, you may not have felt that way a moment before that or even when that statement was said, but I would have felt, "Boy, these guys really trust their leader because they're speaking directly, and openly and honestly confronting you, and knowing that they're not going to be punished or reprimanded." What I also value in the chaos is that people are speaking. Sometimes people say to me, "This is just a gripe session." Well, it may become a gripe session if it goes on and on and on and we have meeting after meeting after meeting, but a lot of times what might be interpreted as a gripe session is just this: "I'm going to put my cards on the table now and tell you exactly what I feel, so I won't go out in the hallway later and talk about you. I'm saying it right here and getting it out in the open."

> | Principal: | What heightened my level of frustration was that I was trying to share a process with them and they were not buying into it. |
> |---|---|
> | Trainer: | A lot of times what I feel might be interpreted as a gripe session is just this: "I'm going to put my cards on the table now and tell you exactly what I feel, so I won't go out in the hallway later and talk about you. I'm saying it right here and getting it out in the open." |

When a problem has been building up for a long time, speaking about it this way for the first time can seem very disruptive to the task. In the long run, though, we begin to realize, "You might put out a memo as the principal, and if I have a question or a concern about it, now I know I don't have to go gripe in a teacher's room. I can go to Jeff and say, 'Hey, Jeff: What's the problem?' You respond, and I say, 'Oh. Okay.' and I walk away feeling all right because I know you're trying to be reasonable and fair with me and hear me out." Has that been your experience, that over the long run the feelings calm down?

JEFFERY GERMAN: People became very relaxed telling me whatever they wanted to say. That helped tremendously because it gave us an opportunity to jointly plan and put programs in place for students.

PAT HOWLEY: And then we can be more cognitive. We can be more rational and focus on children because we've cleared the deck of all of our personal adult agenda items. "I don't have to fight authority"—if I still even have authority issues—"because the authority figure really doesn't want to fight with me. He wants to work with me."

JEFFERY GERMAN: I can say that's how Comer helped me introspectively. I recall making a presentation and having in the audience teachers from a school where I had once been principal. I told them, "You will hear a different Jeff German from the one you heard when we worked together," because I had been one of those it's-going-to-be-my-way-or-no-way principals. And going back and talking about how I had behaved broadened my perspective on where I was trying to go. The teachers came up to me afterward and said, "Oh, you sound so different!" And I said, "Let's call it a revelation!" It's something that I went through. I had to decide: What is the most effective way to mobilize staff to the cause of children? I use that same approach when talking about teachers and relationships. It's got to come from within. You've got to realize that first of all there are some things that you've got to address and then change. When I share that with teachers and in presentations, I tell them, "I am a person who has not always been this way. Don't think that a program that focuses on relationships and trust can't happen. I know it can happen, because it happened to me."

PAT HOWLEY: Don't you also think that you became a principal because of personal needs? Perhaps you saw that there were better ways of running a school than the ways you experienced when you were a teacher. Did you want to get into a position of power and control so you could make things better?

JEFFERY GERMAN: Yes. My intentions may have been goodhearted in nature. I had to hone my skills to make things right.

PAT HOWLEY: The intentions are good, and it also has to do with personalities and styles of leadership. Right?

JEFFERY GERMAN: Part of the metamorphosis that I underwent occurred because of a session that I had with you at the SDP Principals' Academy. The session on Myers-Briggs Type Indicators® provided me with an opportunity to look at myself and start thinking about my own personality type. What was so intriguing is that what I learned, I knew, even though I didn't know how to express it. I knew I had to make some adjustments. Being task oriented is fine. But how do you handle yourself while being task oriented? How do you differentiate between being task oriented and process oriented? After I started learning the different personality types of others around me, I was in a better position to make necessary adjustments when I interacted with them.

PAT HOWLEY: We know that people with certain personality types are attracted to being a principal or being a leader. On the Myers-Briggs chart, these types are in the four corners. There are 16 types on the chart, and the highest percentage of leaders is described by the traits in the four corners. (Editors' note: See Figure 12.4 in the next chapter.)

The Comer Process asks principals to work differently from their natural style and behave in the collaborative styles that are more typical of personality types represented in the middle of the chart—the more intuitive and feeling and perceiving types, whereas many times leaders are of the sensing, thinking, and judging types. They have to make decisions. They have to think things through, and they have to pay attention to detail. And they have to behave like extroverts. So we're asking principals to make a dramatic shift in how they lead, and that's a difficult transition.

I also think there's a need on the part of the staff for you to be an old-fashioned principal: "I don't want to make the decision. I don't want to take the responsibility. I don't want it to be shared responsibility. I would rather have it be your responsibility." So we are sometimes going against the flow because both of us, at some unconscious level, want it to go back to the way it used to be.

MICHAEL BEN-AVIE: Reflecting on my own frustration with SDP processes, I'm aware that sometimes I sit at meetings and think, "Let's just make a decision already! Tell me what to do and I'll do it because I'm such a good soldier. Okay? I don't need this chaos!"

PAT HOWLEY: Well, I feel the same way a lot of times, and I'm at the other end of the spectrum: I like ambiguity, and I know that creativity comes out of a lot of voices being heard. But I get impatient if we do that for too long. Particularly in schools, we need a more structured process.

I'll give you one example of that: Sometimes at a faculty meeting the principal gives out all the information and the teachers are sitting there listening. Then they want "collaboration," so they say to the faculty, "What do you think?" Then 100 faculty members try to have a discussion, and it's chaos. I just want to say, "Let's get on with it. Make a decision." So I suggest to a principal, "Why don't you have a faculty meeting where you group people by grade level or you group them by subject matter and you say, 'Here are the five points I want to make. This is what I think we ought to do. Now sit and talk with your people. Write out your reactions to that on cards. I'm going to collect the cards. I'm going to think about it, and I'm going to make my recommendations on a final decision, and if anybody has any concern, put it on a card and get it back to me, and I'll revise it one more time, and then it's on with it.'" To me, that's still a collaborative process.

JEFFERY GERMAN: Before I became a Comer principal, I would have said, "That's just too time-consuming. *This* is what we're going to do." And for Michael, that would have been okay. He would have left the meeting knowing what had been discussed; there were certain things he had to do; he would have done them, and moved on. For others, it would have heightened their level of frustration. They wouldn't have understood or bought in, they would have wanted some say in the ideas being discussed. But now, we run everything through the subcommittee structure, and I trust the subcommittee members to give us some solutions that we can deal with at the SPMT level. If the SPMT approves the subcommittee solutions, then we take it to the faculty. Now that I have made the adjustment, all those steps are okay with me.

PAT HOWLEY: Right. At one extreme, discussion can be pure chaos with no end in sight, and at the other, it can be totally controlled and directed by the leader. SDP permits people to build something in the middle that guides discussion. We still have input and buy-in, but the whole process is guided and structured.

MICHAEL BEN-AVIE: My deep appreciation for your thoughts. I hear you. However, I still feel some resistance. Consider teachers or administrators who contribute to the implementation of the Comer Process in their schools by tracking data on achievement, absenteeism, mobility, et cetera. They have their clearly defined areas of accountability and responsibility. At certain meetings, there may be topics that are outside of their sphere of action. They may feel that the discussions pull them away from their primary responsibilities and areas of strength. I know this feeling very well.

PAT HOWLEY: You're wondering, "Can I really make any significant contribution to the content?"

MICHAEL BEN-AVIE: The agenda should have been set in a way that the need for my contribution would have been clear.

JEFFERY GERMAN: Well, even when your specialty area is not the direct focus of discussion, we need you.

MICHAEL BEN-AVIE: If you want me to be a passive observer taking it all in, I'm willing to play that role. But you've got to tell me what you want from me. I feel I don't understand that sometimes. And that's why I get so frustrated. Does that make sense?

PAT HOWLEY: We expect you to be an active group member and we don't have to make that clear each time.

JEFFERY GERMAN: You know that was some of the feedback that we got from recent SDP 102 Leadership Academy participants. I can recall reading one of the evaluation sheets on which the person had written that it would be helpful that when we got to a particular module we should have been working more within our specialty groups, i.e., our school-level groups. In other words, I'm a secondary education person. If people at my table were all in secondary education, I might see this discussion in a different light. But as it stands now, the people at my table are from K–5, 6–8, maybe one other high school person, a principal, and a person from a central office. So I think that level of frustration was clearly documented by whoever wrote that comment.

MICHAEL BEN-AVIE: And how would you respond to that, Pat?

PAT HOWLEY: There are two points I want to make. The first point is that you talk about content, but maybe your contribution could be to the process because your frustration could help us to speed up the process without short-circuiting it. We've still got to work things through, but we need someone there to say, "Well, are we ready to go on to the next thing?" Also,

Researcher:	Sometimes I sit at these meetings and think, "Let's just make a decision already! Tell me what to do and I'll do it because I'm such a good soldier. Okay? I don't need this chaos!"
Trainer:	Well, I feel the same way a lot of times, and I'm at the other end of the spectrum. . . . At one extreme, discussion can be pure chaos with no end in sight, and at the other, it can be totally controlled and directed by the leader. . . . Maybe your contribution could be to process because your frustration could help us to speed up the process without short-circuiting it. Remember, whatever my particular area is— my turf—I need to see connections to the big picture. Otherwise, we have what's called fragmentation: Our work disintegrates into fragments, and people end up working against each other.
Principal:	When you know the purpose of the meeting and clarify the agenda, you then determine the appropriate audience, or group composition. There are times we need everyone and times we meet in specialty groups. Even when we meet in specialty groups or subcommittees we still need to bring everyone back together. And when we do so, we must remember that the subcommittee group decisions were recommendations. At the larger meeting there has to be a climate in which people feel comfortable speaking out.

someone like you might raise points about the key elements of the process such as, "What are the four major concerns we have about this issue?" or "What are the three problems we're trying to tackle right now, and is there a way that we can just articulate those?" Someone who is task oriented tends to bring the focus back to the task. And if we become too task oriented and we haven't heard everyone, there's someone like me that usually comes along and says, "Hey, wait a minute: We haven't heard from Jeff yet. What do you think about this, Jeff?"

So the value of having different people on the content side is that we've still included people who are more task oriented or more content oriented. And if you have the role of notetaker, let's say, you might say, "Well, I don't know if I've got all the points that you mentioned. I have three points that you've listed so far in my notes . . ." and then somebody says, "Oh, the other thing we said was this: . . ." When you raise the question of what we had in our notes, we all become a little more focused not just on having a discussion but on going back to the task of why we're having this discussion in the first place.

Another point about this is that there are times where you could just have a focus group. But there are other times when looking at the global picture and having everyone connected to the big picture is what helps each one do his or her small piece. Because remember, whatever my particular area is—my turf—I need to see connections to the big picture. Otherwise, we have what's called fragmentation: Our work disintegrates into fragments, and people end up working against each other. I think that's what's happened a lot in our society. For example, I once asked a computer specialist about the Internet and he said, "Well, that's not my area of expertise," and so I had to call in 15 different experts to work on my computer. It has become so complex that no one knows the big picture.

JEFFERY GERMAN: When you know the purpose of the meeting and clarify the agenda, you then determine the appropriate audience, or group composition. There are times we need everyone and times we meet in specialty groups. Even when we meet in specialty groups or subcommittees we still need to bring everyone back together. And when we do so, we must remember that the subcommittee group decisions were recommendations. At the larger meeting there has to be a climate in which people feel comfortable speaking out.

PAT HOWLEY: Absolutely. That's a great point.

MICHAEL BEN-AVIE: I agree. And also it seems to me that that's what happened at the faculty meeting where there was fragmentation. You had your elective teachers feeling fragmented from this whole schoolwide tutoring program. So how did you address that?

JEFFERY GERMAN: The main thing was to give them an opportunity to share that. I could have walked into that faculty meeting and said, "Based on what came out of the leadership team, this is what we're going to do for Level I and Level II students." Then I would have people sitting there saying, "I don't think that's fair to me. I'm a Spanish teacher. Nobody asked me how I feel about it." Instead, we put the issue on the table and said, "This is what the leadership team agreed that we would like to do to make sure that our achievement results improve for Level I and Level II students. How do you feel about it?" Forty-five minutes later, we were still listening to each other and the main thing was we were still learning.

PAT HOWLEY:

And so you become a facilitator of their learning from each other by listening. They could see that the principal thinks it's important enough to listen. Then other parts of the school are going to listen as well because they see you modeling listening. And then they may learn something.

JEFFERY GERMAN:

I think you hit it on the head a while ago. Somebody said, "Hey, we don't vote here." Somebody said, in effect, "You know, here's the principal, and he's willing to sit here and listen. I think I feel comfortable enough to be able to say to him, 'That's not the process that we want to use to bring closure to this.'"

PAT HOWLEY:

It brings trust. Right? It builds trust so that they can say the things that need to be said. And it can get worked through and worked out .

JEFFERY GERMAN:

And it didn't stop after that. They felt very comfortable coming to the office to talk through problems or

> The Comer Process builds trust so that they can say the things that need to be said. And it can get worked through and worked out.

doing that when we were in meetings. That carried over in meetings with parents.

PAT HOWLEY:

And that's where it has to do with the metaphor of the container. Because what you've done is say, "We're going to have this discussion here right now, and I'm going to listen to it." So now it's contained by your being there modeling how to hear different viewpoints. You're really saying to everyone, "Each viewpoint is important and it's going to be heard." So if it's spoken openly, it's talked out openly rather than talked about outside of the container. (Editors' note: See Chapter 10.)

JEFFERY GERMAN:

Perhaps a way to extend that metaphor would be this: You're bringing in an empty container. Because everybody is involved, you're not really filling up the container yourself, putting the cap on, and saying, "This is the way it's going to be done." If I want to use the container metaphor, I'd want to make sure that I understand that there is room to add to what's already in the container, and also that I must make sure that the container is still open and not closed.

PAT HOWLEY: Yes. As the principal, you are a container. And when the SPMT brings issues to the faculty and presents the issues, then at that point the SPMT is the container for the rest of the school. And they're saying, "Everyone in the school can dump everything into this container, and we're going to hold it. We're going to listen to you, we're going to listen to you, we're going to listen to you. There will be disagreements, and we're not dismissing anyone's points. We're holding them all in the mix in the container to see what will make sense."

If the container isn't there or if it's got holes in it, then people won't be able to understand, and they won't have trust. They won't speak openly at meetings. Instead, they'll go talk to their buddies, and valuable information and creative ideas will be lost. But when the container is open and well made and well used, then you and the SPMT can say in your own meetings, for example, "Okay. Look: We've collected all these cards because we asked people not only to share their ideas but also to write them down so we could capture them." Then you have a discussion and the SPMT starts sorting out all the data. Then you can go back to the faculty and say, "This is the sense we made of all your comments, and these are the decisions we are proposing." You've created a structure: It's a container for people to go into and process ideas and determine what action steps to take in the best interests of the students.

READ MORE ABOUT . . .

For information on the Myers-Briggs and its use in SDP leadership academies, see Chapter 12 in this volume, "It's All About Effective Relationships: Frameworks for Understanding Ourselves and Others."

For information on the metaphor of the container, see Chapter 10 in this volume, "A Team Approach to Educational Change."

12

It's All About Effective Relationships

Frameworks for
Understanding Ourselves and Others

J. Patrick Howley

Nothing can be accomplished on school teams when the members don't respect or work well with each other—and anything can be accomplished when they do. SDP's director of Teaching and Adult Development offers several ways in which to nurture good relationships on teams by (1) making sense of our own and others' motivations, behavior, and personality types, (2) giving and receiving feedback appropriately, and (3) developing well-founded trust in team processes.

This chapter sets forth two key relationship frameworks that can be used as tools to understand, support, and develop healthy relationships. These frameworks are (1) "windows" to understanding ourselves and others, and (2) models of personality types to understand patterns of human behavior. By examining these frameworks, it is possible to see beyond the complexity of human relationships and to harness their power in order to support effective change and school improvement. These frameworks provide a guide for creating healthy and productive relationships. By developing basic understandings of people and the ways they relate, it is possible to effectively address current and potential problems. Before discussing the frameworks, I will begin by creating a picture of the nature of relationships.

Recently, I called a computer company to request technical assistance. The support person asked me what was wrong and what I saw on my screen. She promptly told me to take a series of steps on the computer. Then she told me we would have to wait a moment. As I waited, we chatted briefly. Something else came up on my screen. She paused, and then said, "Okay, now hit the enter key and another menu should pop up." She continued her directions and then asked me to wait again, saying that this action would take a few moments as well. While I was waiting, I said that I wished I had a job like hers—where someone could tell me what was wrong in clear and precise terms. Then I could tell them exactly the steps to take to fix the problem.

Unlike working with computer problems—where we can lay out a step-by-step formula to solve the problem—the issues that we face in schools are more complex, involving the interplay of issues of trust, power, self-esteem, miscommunications, cultural differences, and role differences, to name a few. The human condition and the interactions between and among adults are considerably less predictive than computers and infinitely more complicated. Nevertheless, human relationships are the cornerstone of school change and school improvement. The relationships in our schools can either support or hinder efforts at improvement and growth.

To illustrate the nature of the complexity of relationships I will share a scenario culled from a number of similar conversations, relationships, and work that I have conducted with principals in Comer schools throughout the country. It is intended to highlight points relevant to building effective relationships through the frameworks.

A HUMAN RELATIONSHIP SCENARIO

The new principal, Fred Rivas (pseudonym), and I sat in his office together. He was perplexed. "How could potentially excellent teachers end up like this?" he asked, not looking for an answer from me. His discouragement was palpable.

After Rivas had been in the school system for 10 years as an elementary school principal, the superintendent had asked him to take on the challenge of managing the middle school. One principal had been there for 19 years. After that principal had retired, the school had four principals in the next three years. Rivas was now the next new principal. He was most concerned about a core group of aging faculty who seemed sour, angry, sullen, and bitter.

Rivas had received a grant to start the School Development Program (SDP). A few years earlier, he and I had discovered that we had similar interests in spirituality, development, psychology, and of course, education. Our work started when he shared with me that he wanted a sounding board to help him reflect on himself, his role, and the needs of his school. He wanted to be able to talk with someone who was outside the school system, someone who had a neutral perspective. He had asked me to meet with him on a regular basis to think and plan.

"I have been in every classroom, and this faculty is smart," he said to me on this cold January afternoon. "They are good teachers and they could be excellent. At this time in their careers, they could be master teachers—stars of the teaching profession. They could and should be teaching courses in the teacher prep program at our local college. However, anything I propose to them for improving the school is rejected. They only complain. They fight with each other over petty issues. Worst of all, they don't seem to enjoy being with and teaching children. How could they have gotten to this point? And how am I going to get them to be motivated to do Comer?"

Earlier in the year, Rivas had asked me to meet with the staff and interview them individually and in small groups. In the interviews, I had learned that the differences among staff members were readily apparent. For example, as in all middle schools, teachers were teaching at different grade levels (sixth, seventh, and eighth grades). And of course, they were teaching different subjects. However, what was somewhat different in this school was the age range of teachers, from newcomers to 30-year veterans. Most of the staff were either first- or second-year teachers or very seasoned veterans. Teaching philosophies were also very different. Teachers who had formerly taught at the elementary level focused on kids, teachers who had formerly taught at the high school level focused on subject matter, and teachers with the true middle school philosophy tended to see school as being about developmental transition time for children. In addition, some teachers hung on to the traditional philosophy of the junior high concept—preparing students for high school.

These differences surfaced around the following relationship-based issues:

• *Conflict with authority:* The teachers complained: "He [the principal] should be in charge and not try to collaborate so much." "He doesn't seem to have a sense of direction. He wants us to make the decisions for him." "It's about time we got a leader who will listen to us. But he listens too much to parents." "He says we can make more decisions collaboratively, but we know he has already decided to do Comer. The principal's decision-making process is not collaborative."

• *Trust:* The teachers lamented: "You can't trust anyone in this building." "I hear stories all the time. There is too much gossip."

• *Low morale:* The teachers voiced discouragement: "There is too much negativity in this building." "The veteran staff members are too critical and don't give any idea a chance." "New teachers think they know it all and get favored by the principal." "I am too old, I guess. I see the same ideas get recycled in a new package. But this principal won't stay, and we will have to live with whatever he started." "As special education, we are forgotten. Our needs and concerns are not addressed." "Music and art are considered the unimportant subjects by other teachers." "As a teacher aide, I don't think my opinion matters." "A long time ago we would get together on a regular basis outside of school. Now, few show up even for our holiday party."

• *Communication:* The teachers asserted: "We don't always know what is going on." "We are told at the last minute we have to show up at a meeting."

Needless to say, the principal felt discouraged and unable to move the faculty in any positive direction. Issues of blaming, gossiping, and lack of collaboration had led to a climate that left him feeling defeated as a school leader.

MAKING SENSE OF RELATIONSHIPS

Although the story recounted above gives only a brief description of the types of issues that teachers raised, the power of these voices is too often omnipresent in school environments.

Tensions

The types of issues that these statements reveal have inherent tensions that frequently exist in relationships, specifically:

- *In versus Out:* Some people are perceived as part of the "in" crowd, with a strong relationship and alliance with the principal, while others look in from the outside and see the principal identifying "favorites."

- *Personal versus Professional:* Often teachers feel overwhelmed by change and pressure (e.g., to raise test scores). They feel either isolated from each other because of so much work or resentful that they do not have time for a personal life.

- *Change versus Locus of Control:* Individuals perceive that they are part of change, or that change is "done unto" them. In the scenario described above, everything was changing so fast that the staff felt a loss of control over their professional lives (e.g., "I'm not unwilling to change; it's just that change is being shoved down our throats").

- *Personal Decision Making versus Organizational Power:* Individuals feel the organization is controlling their lives and experiences. For example, the changes demanded are coming from arenas that are external to the classroom, such as the central office and the state. Teachers perceive that they have little say in what needs to happen for kids.

Evolving Stages

I shared with Rivas the notion that relationships in schools typically evolve through three stages of development: dependence, independence, and interdependence.

Dependence

At this stage a teacher new to the school is dependent on others (e.g., the school secretary, principal, and other teachers) for help in learning even the basics, such as where to park, how to use the phone system, what forms need to be completed, understanding the curriculum, discipline procedures, how they will be evaluated, and so on. Adults tend not to like being dependent and may struggle with many uncomfortable feelings at this stage.

Independence

When teachers have been in a school for a number of years they now "know the ropes." They have learned both the formal and informal rules, and they know the personalities of their colleagues and leaders. Life in the school becomes predictable because they know, in general, what to expect from their principal, the parents, and their students. People find a niche and this becomes their comfort zone, where they gain confidence by developing skills, practicing, and being in a consistent environment that supports their growth.

Yet, there are so many changes occurring now in schools: new programs and expectations of teachers that they will "leave no child behind," students having to meet standards on the state testing program, new administrators at both the central office and their schools, retiring colleagues, influx of new teachers, accountability through new evaluation procedures, new training in curriculum, new teaching methods, and whole school reform efforts. Many teachers respond with, "Another thing we have to do? I can't keep up." Having all these changes occur simultaneously throws even the veteran back to the dependence stage, resulting in feelings of discomfort, being overwhelmed, resistant, and being out of control.

Interdependence

At the interdependent stage teachers realize that we (parents, teachers, and administration) are all in this together and we need one another to succeed with children. No one has all the answers and no one can do it alone. At this stage, teachers are able to feel a degree of comfort despite realizing that they do not know everything. They will ask questions, and they will answer the questions of others when they can.

It is the responsibility of each individual to work to gain personal confidence to progress through these stages, and indeed, to go back and forth between stages when appropriate. It is also the responsibility of the school system to create a culture and context in which the adults develop all of their potential so that they can use their natural gifts to foster the growth of children.

Creating Strength From Diversity

SDP is designed to help schools progress to this most advanced stage, interdependence, at which point all of a school's diversity becomes its strength. SDP achieves this by valuing each voice within the school: child, parent, teacher, support staff, and administration. (A Comer school recognizes that each member of the school community has a view to contribute.) What supports the development of the faculty and allows them to keep their focus on children is their adherence to the three guiding principles: no-fault, consensus, and collaboration. By committing to (1) solve problems without focusing on who's to blame; (2) make decisions, when appropriate, by consensus; and (3) work in collaborative relationships, the faculty experiences a sense of community. In many schools, when faculty members become paralyzed in their work, what needs to be addressed is an additional commitment by the adults to learn the skills that will help them live the guiding principles with one another, and to develop themselves in order to develop children.

Understanding Our Own Behavior in Relationships

When Rivas started to talk about the previous principal who had been at the school so long, he talked about the faculty's dependence on him and the mixed feelings the faculty seemed to have about him. The conversation triggered something I learned about relationships from Eric Berne (1964) in a book on the subject of transactional analysis. The brief overview of the concept is this: At any age, each person has within himself or herself a "parent," an "adult," and a "child." When one person acts toward a second person "from their child," it tends to activate the "parent" within the other person. And vice versa; when someone acts as a "parent" toward another, this will tend to activate the "child" within the other person.

This response from either side could be positive or negative, but one important point is this: People are often not aware of this transaction. The real problem is that relationships become dysfunctional when people are not interacting from the adult in themselves to the adult in the person with whom they are in a relationship. This becomes even more critical when the relationship involves an authority figure. In cases such as these, the adult/child relationships that occurred in their families of origin can easily become reenacted without either side being aware of it.

True adult-to-adult communications are direct, honest, open, and straightforward. Each person takes responsibility by asking questions if there is not enough clarity. Each may openly state what the potential problems might be in a proposal someone is suggesting and then offer solutions or help if it is needed. There is little dependence, game playing, being a victim, complaining, defensiveness, fighting, or the like.

If Rivas expected his staff to act in more adult and responsible ways, then he needed to make sure that his own behavior came from the adult in him—not the parent in him. Scolding, praising, lecturing, taking care of, or being fatherly in any way would only activate the child response from his teachers, and that response would probably not be constructive or helpful. It would tend to bring out the qualities of rebellious child, victim child, or passive child in his staff.

Moreover, if we return to the relationship-based issues identified earlier, it is clear that a lack of trust was a major factor impacting the relationships and development of the staff. At another meeting with Rivas, I had shared with him that there were two issues related to trusting relationships:

- *Does each teacher trust himself or herself?* Do they trust their own thoughts, feelings, intuitions, perceptions, and judgments?

- *Do teachers trust each other?* Do they trust that others can be counted on, will listen, will respect and honor their point of view, and will try to see the situation by putting themselves in the other's shoes?

If trust is the foundation, then the process of supporting change in schools must begin with asking the question, "How do we develop trust when we are at present in an untrusting environment?" This question leads to the discussion of the first framework for understanding relationships, the Jo-hari Window (Luft & Ingham, 1963).

RELATIONSHIP FRAMEWORK 1: THE JO-HARI WINDOW

In Chapter 10, "A Team Approach to Educational Change," I covered the following points:

- Among the concerns that people bring into their school are these: Who am I? How do I relate to others? Do I have any influence, power, or impact on others?
- People's concerns in schools need to be held and supported within a strong container that enables everyone to keep their focus on the development of children.
- There is always a need for reflection.
- Feedback informs our reflection process.

A Framework for Developing Trust and Healthy Relationships in Schools

To take these ideas further, imagine that people in schools have a window that they can hold psychologically in front of other people. In Leadership Training 101, I explain to participants that the window is called the "Jo-hari Window" because it is named after the people who created the concept, Joseph Luft and Harry Ingham (1963).

The Jo-hari Window is a means to help individuals understand some aspects of the dynamics of relationships. It fosters an understanding of the importance and place of trusting relationships. Effective, constructive relationships help us to build strong, cohesive bonds that ensure that teams stick together through the difficult times—the times of intense differences and conflict. Trust is the glue that keeps relationships together. If relationships are not built on trust, then they can easily fall apart. It is the trust among all the adults in the community that creates the strong container needed for children so that they know what is expected of them by adults in the school community.

This psychological framework can be seen in Figure 12.1, the Jo-hari Window. Pane D represents the unconscious part of us, unknown to ourselves and others. I have started with Pane D because in this discussion we will not need to address it further. However, it is important to note that people are often not conscious of the interactions that take place between themselves and others.

Public Self and Private Self

Pane A represents the part of us that is known to ourselves and known to, or easily knowable by, others. This is called the Public Self or Coffee Talk window. Let's say I come into a school as a substitute teacher, and we meet for the first time in the faculty room. You might ask, "Who are you today?" meaning, who are you subbing for? We might ask questions like, "How long have you been doing this?" "Do you like being a substitute teacher?" I am open to and would easily answer the questions, and, in fact, appreciate your interest in me. This is coffee talk. It is a way to get to know one another and communicate on a regular basis. Faculty in a school may remain at a coffee talk level of openness and make exchanges like, "You're on duty in the hallway today, and I'm on tomorrow." "How was your vacation?" or "I had a great weekend. How was yours?" This type of conversation pretty much stays at the surface level. It may be sufficient communication to enable staff to work together. For school relationships to move to a more effective level of communication, however, we need to consider the value of entering into the behaviors described in the remaining two Panes: C and B.

The difficulty with talking coffee talk all the time is that although it is possible to maintain a functional connection to one another, when important issues surface it is easy to avoid them. Individuals play it safe by not taking the risky steps of addressing the issues directly, and they therefore do not gain the potential rewards found in the remaining two panes. It is understandable why most people remain in the safety of the coffee talk pane: There is too much risk involved. Yet, if the goal is to grow and develop into a cohesive faculty, it becomes essential to put our cards on the table. There is risk—yes, but there are also potentially high payoffs in the remaining two panes: C, the Private Self, and B, the Blind Self.

Pane C is information about ourselves that we know but others do not. It's as if I have a sign on my front lawn that says "Private Property. Keep Out!" We all have the right to our privacy, and yet the question is always there with us: How much do

Figure 12.1 The Jo-hari Window

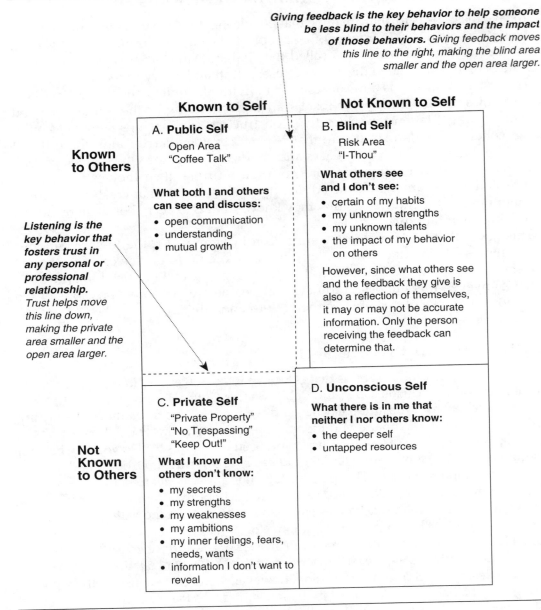

SOURCE: Adapted from Luft and Ingham (1963).

I tell others about myself, both personally and professionally? Some people feel that if they reveal too much, even about their professional selves, it leaves them vulnerable. If someone shares, for example, that they are having difficulty with a child in their class, they might fear that others would perceive them as not being able to handle disruptive children. And of course, others may actually have that perception.

The value to people of sharing more about their professional selves is that more information is available and, therefore, there is less chance of a miscommunication. Most problems that schools have are rooted in communication problems.

If one teacher has learned what has worked well with a child and another teacher is struggling, it only makes sense that they share. If a teacher has gone to a workshop and learned some effective teaching strategies, it is beneficial to the school for that teacher to share the new knowledge with colleagues.

Facilitating Trust

In the SDP Leadership Academy 101 I ask, "What would it take for me to open up to you—to move information about myself from the Private Self up into the Public Self?" The answer is usually "trust." I then ask, "What can you do—actually do in your behavior—that will establish or create trust?" This is more difficult to answer, but I sometimes get very insightful responses. The primary answer that I look for (it is not the only right answer) is this: "I can listen."

Before I address the fourth pane of the Johari Window (Pane B, the Blind Self), I need to elaborate further upon how we build trusting relationships through listening.

Rogers (1980) comments that three conditions (see sidebar) constitute the "growth promoting climate," and they apply "whether we are speaking of the relationship between therapist and client, parent and child, leader and group, teacher and student, or administrator and staff." Rogers goes on to say that people who experience the three facilitative conditions move consistently toward having the following habits of behavior and mind:

> Carl Rogers, who has written extensively about listening, uses what he calls a person-centered approach. Three core conditions are necessary, he said, for a trusting relationship, and for growth and change to occur in that relationship. These core conditions or qualities or attitudes are (1) being genuine or real, (2) unconditional positive regard (prizing, acceptance, or caring), and (3) being able to demonstrate accurate empathetic understanding.

- They are more open to experience, more aware of the here and now, less defensive, less rigid in their beliefs, and more tolerant of ambiguity.
- They are self-trusting, relying on their experiences when making decisions.
- They look more toward themselves for answers instead of looking outside for validation.
- They are more willing to continue growing and learning.

A relationship built on these conditions creates trust. By trust I mean not only trusting the person in the relationship but also deeply trusting the very process of growth. Rogers talked many times about how as a young child he observed potato stalks growing in his basement. The conditions were not right, yet the stalks continued to grow, however grotesquely, toward the only light available in the dark, damp cellar. They grew toward a condition they needed, sunlight.

Karen Horney (1950), a psychologist, said something similar:

> You need not, and in fact cannot, teach an acorn to grow into an oak tree, but when given a chance, its intrinsic potentialities will develop. Similarly, the human individual, given a chance, tends to develop his particular human potentialities. . . . In short, he will grow substantially un-diverted toward self-realization. (p. 17)

This means trusting that deep within each person lies an expert that becomes a foundation for experience, making meanings and decisions. When people are less defensive, they listen better and they learn more. How do we create the conditions in which people can be less defensive? How can we create the psychologically safe conditions for human beings? Listening deeply seems to be the primary way to create the conditions that both Horney and Rogers talk about that build trust in relationships.

The Blind Self

The final Pane is B, the Blind Self. This is information that is known to others but is not known to the person. A superintendent once presented SDP to two schools in his district. He only wanted to give them some information about the model so they could make their own decision. When I went to one of the schools, the principal and the teachers said that they "*had* to do Comer." Although the superintendent had presented SDP as an option, they *knew* that they must do it.

When I met with the superintendent, he was shocked that the school administration and staff had received the information that way. He was blind to the fact that in his role of superintendent, his act of presenting the model to the school would be seen as a demand of the school. The key skill that people develop to address this blind side is learning to give and receive feedback. If someone at the school had taken the risk of telling the superintendent that it appeared to them that he was telling them to implement the Comer Process, he would have been able to respond and clarify his intentions.

People are not always aware of how their behavior affects others at the levels of thoughts, feelings, and behaviors. There are sometimes very subtle behaviors that the always-observing mind picks up and reacts to, yet initially the conscious mind is not aware of them. That is the inner feeling that says, "Something is not quite right here." If we reflect on it more we might pinpoint what we have seen, explore what we think and feel, and then risk sharing it—give feedback.

Feedback in the Jo-hari Window

What, then, is feedback? What is the purpose of using this process? And how can people best use feedback skills to improve their schools?

Feedback is the information component of a process of growth and development. In this process, a person shares his or her perceptions about another person or a situation. The feedback itself has three parts: (1) a description of observed behavior, (2) a description of the impact of that behavior on others, and (3) a description of feelings and thoughts. The behavior of the person giving the feedback has a powerful influence on the outcome of the process. The more the person offering feedback demonstrates Rogers's three core conditions, the more likely it is that the feedback will be considered to be constructive.

The purpose of practicing sound feedback skills is to

- strengthen the processes of consensus, collaboration, and no-fault
- provide opportunities to give differing viewpoints of children
- strengthen our commitment to faithful replication of the Comer model
- provide a constructive way to bring issues and problems to the surface so that the problems can be addressed

In the service of promoting effective teamwork, SDP uses facilitators and process observers to ensure that the team meeting honors human relations. The facilitator carefully delineates the context in which feedback is appropriate. At the beginning and end of each meeting, time is devoted to checking in with one another about the process.

The six areas in Comer schools about which feedback is appropriate are the following:

1. leadership

2. facilitation (and other team roles as described on the role cards)

3. living the three guiding principles

4. the six developmental pathways

5. gifts, strengths, and contributions of members in the school

6. what we would like to change about our team to improve it

Figures 12.2 and 12.3 offer specific guidelines for giving and receiving feedback to optimize acceptance and use.

Figure 12.2 Principles of giving individual feedback

1. Make your intent to provide information.

2. Be unemotional as you give information.

3. Be straightforward, descriptive, and specific.

4. Focus on observed behaviors and their observed effect on others.

5. Recognize that you are sharing observations, thoughts, feelings, perceptions, and experiences, and not necessarily true facts.

6. Trust what is experienced, and share it with a conviction that people have a right to share their experience with others.

7. Make a commitment to act in ways that are fully respectful of everyone.

8. Be gentle, sensitive to the feelings of others, and caring.

9. Take the time to discuss the process of giving and receiving feedback in order to clarify misperceptions, miscommunications, and misunderstandings.

10. Share ideas and information rather than give advice.

11. Focus on the value the feedback would have for the receiver rather than your need to give feedback.

12. Focus feedback on what, when, how, where, and not why.

13. Be direct rather than indirect.

14. Be descriptive rather than interpretive.

15. Feedback should be nonevaluative and nonjudgmental.

16. Provide a freedom of choice rather than a pressure to change.

17. The motivation to provide feedback is to help, not attack.

18. Encourage others to solicit feedback rather than impose it.

19. Focus on behavior that can be modified.

SOURCE: Adapted in part from Hanson, P. G. (1975). Giving feedback: An interpersonal skill, in Jones, J. E. & Pfeiffer, W. J. (Eds.), *The 1975 Annual Handbook for Group Facilitators (the fourth annual).* La Jolla, CA: University Associates.

Figure 12.3 Principles for receiving individual feedback

Listen!

Try not to say anything right away.

Let the information soak in.

Think: I don't have to change, and I may not want to or be able to.

Keep in mind that what a person is saying to you is *not* the truth:
It is their *perception*.

Listen to the feedback, even if you don't agree with it.

There might be some valuable information that may help you learn about yourself.

Ask for more information.

Rarely do people give feedback that is easy to hear and understand immediately.

Ask the speaker about his or her intentions.

Sometimes we forget or don't realize that the other person is only trying
to help us improve ourselves.

YOU DON'T HAVE TO CHANGE!!

You will change only if you want to change and only if you can change.

The Jo-hari Window can be a helpful guide for adults who are interested in interacting in a more effective manner. Principal Rivas realized from the Jo-hari Window that although he could not understand the hidden motivations and needs of all staff members (Pane D), he still could encourage his staff to be more open with him and to listen to one another (Pane A). He also could foster community building and team building workshops so that teachers could get to know each other better and create more trusting relationships (moving information from Pane C to Pane A). And finally, he could provide strategic, skillful, nonjudgmental feedback that encouraged his staff (1) to stop to think about what they were doing to each other, and (2) to reflect on what they were doing in the classroom to develop children (Pane B).

Working With Our Awareness of Self and Others

Principal Rivas knew that teachers' ability to change (to develop) children depends on their commitment to their own development. Well-developed adults foster well-developed children. He also knew that changing his teachers would begin with deepening his own awareness of himself. His own professional development included his exterior world of learning (his professional development) to be a good principal. He also attended to his interior work (his personal development), in which he explored his personality and leadership style through the Myers-Briggs® model.

Rivas began slowly and deliberately to create strategies for developing his staff, both as professionals and as persons. He created a team to examine the climate and culture of the school. He asked that team to list their concerns about staff's behavior and children's behavior. They discussed the causes. He asked this team, which later became the school climate subcommittee of the School Planning and Management Team (SPMT), to describe their ideal school. The team slowly began to formulate a direction for development for both the children and the adults along the six developmental pathways. Rivas not only respected differences in his staff, he valued those differences. Through self-awareness work, Rivas became more aware of others and of what they needed from him as a leader. He brought the adults in the building together by being aware of, and then attending to, their developmental needs. He was able to direct their energy to the developmental needs of children.

RELATIONSHIP FRAMEWORK 2: THREE MODELS OF PERSONALITY TYPES—A SHORT COURSE IN UNDERSTANDING PEOPLE

Human beings have an interior life. When we are unaware of this, we cannot see the human beings behind the roles they fill. Whether we are observing a student, parent, teacher, principal, secretary, or social worker, if we look deeper we will see a life full of feelings—zest, anger, joy, resentment, excitement, fear, hope, helplessness, love, sadness, fullness, emptiness, wounds, fond memories, scars from abuse, and a desire to be the best the person can be. Even the strongest of us have a need for hugs, a smile, some warmth, a little recognition, a dose of validation, a firm hand of support, a need for help to tackle what we don't know, an empathetic ear, a reaching out when we have failed or made a mistake. All of us have experienced being confused, frustrated, mistrusted, misunderstood, ignored. None of us has escaped the onslaught of constant change, of having to learn something brand new (like computers and Palm Pilots). We can't get away from feeling that our life is being driven by the dictates of the central office, Board of Education requirements, state mandates, and federal regulations. We seem to be under the microscope of a public that expects more of us yet appreciates little. We in education have been on trial, found guilty, and condemned as incorrigible.

We think, we act, but we also feel. Unless we are forced to, however, most of us give little acknowledgment to our own feelings or to the feelings of others. We forget our own inner life; we can't see it or don't want to recognize it, much less recognize the inner life of someone else. It is too painful to feel our idealism shatter before us. And we certainly do not want to see or hear from someone else's inner life, as it might be a mirror of our own soul. We forget that behind the façade of our professional attitude or our mask of indifference, bitterness, or cynicism, we not only have an interior professional life of feelings, we also have an interior personal life of feelings. These two worlds, the personal and the professional, are inextricably interwoven. We cannot separate one from the other.

We have been taught a certain way to see the world and ourselves by our parents, family, friends, and teachers. We may have been taught that to love ourselves we have to prove ourselves and accomplish something. Or we may have learned disdain for ourselves because we see ourselves as lazy. We may enter the classroom as a beginning teacher with confidence or with trepidation. But, we do feel. And these feelings affect how we think—how we think about school, children, teaching, learning, and ourselves.

We may be experienced teachers who are just tired sometimes. We don't have the energy we once did, and we may fear our own aging process and even resent the youthful innocence of others. We may sense that our opinions are not as valued as they once were. We may even feel like orphans: abandoned, ignored after we have dedicated all of our youthful energy to our school and classroom. The trust and confidence we once felt in ourselves and for others have been replaced, first, by the hurt of betrayal, and then by disappointment, anger, and a warrior-like need to attack. We may be principals who feel caught in the middle between the needs and demands of children, parents, teachers, and the central office. We may be parents feeling overwhelmed with making a living, raising our children, and striving to make a better life for ourselves and our family.

Not only do we forget that people have an inner life, but we also forget that each of us has had to deal with the everyday traumas of life: not earning enough money, losing jobs, differences and conflicts with loved ones, losses, mistakes made, illnesses, accidents, and deaths. We carry all of that around each and every moment. It affects how we see and feel about this world in which we all live.

Developing an awareness of self is the first step in developing relationships. In order to understand others and to develop more meaningful and effective relationships, it is critical to begin by developing a deeper understanding of self. What follows is a brief summary, or short course, of models for understanding self and others. Teams using the models can (1) develop new insights, (2) begin to open up to one another, and (3) invite and receive feedback that will promote healthy and effective interpersonal relationships in schools.

Developing this awareness is not about doing therapy or delving deeply into our own psyches or those of others. What these three models have in common are characterizations of different types of people that are concrete, accurate, and descriptive rather than judgmental. These models can support people as they begin to understand and respect differences that they encounter as they work together. This understanding enables collaborative work and creates a no-fault environment.

The behavior of others may seem pretty random and unpredictable, yet if viewed through the right lens it begins to be quite easily understood. "We then can more easily live in a no-fault way with others because," as Isabel Myers (Myers with Myers, 1995) has said:

> All too often, others with whom we come in contact do not reason as we reason, or do not value the things we value, or are not interested in what interests us. The merit of the theory . . . is that it enables us to expect specific personality differences in particular people and to cope with the people and the differences in a constructive way. Briefly, the theory is that much seemingly chance variation in human behavior is not due to chance; it is in fact the logical result of a few basic, observable differences in mental functioning. (p. 1)

Although people can and do change, there are certain energies, ways of collecting information, reflecting on the information, and making decisions that are integral to individuals. Knowing about self and others creates an ability to build bridges among individuals. This awareness can create relationships that balance and complement individual strengths and weaknesses. It then becomes possible to learn from people who previously may have seemed to be a threat. And they, in turn, learn about us.

Education is about people—children and the adults who work with them. The nature of the relationships that have developed within a school may appear to have little logic. In a most beautiful way, sometimes, there is a logic and it is understandable. The brief descriptions found on the following pages point out this logic. The help that these models provide can be tapped by exploring each of them in more depth. Our short course will provide a brief overview of three models for looking at yourself and others: the Myers-Briggs Type Indicator®, the Enneagram, and Archetypes.

The Myers-Briggs Type Indicator

The Myers-Briggs Type Indicator® (MBTI®) is a self-report questionnaire (indicator) that helps people identify which of 16 personality types is most like them (see Figure 12.4). It has been used for more than 50 years.

The descriptions are nonjudgmental, helping people to see their natural and unique gifts. The descriptions of the 16 types come from the variations of the four variables of opposite qualities: Introvert and Extravert, Sensing and Intuition, Thinking and Feeling, and Perceiving and Judging.

Briefly, Introverts tend to reflect first, before acting, while Extraverts will act first, and then reflect on the action they took. High Sensing people tend to pay more attention to details, while Intuitives (we use the letter *N* for Intuition and the letter *I* for Introverts) tend to look at the big picture and how things are connected or related. Thinking Types on the MBTI tend to look at the world more logically to help them make decisions, while the Feeling Types tend to make decisions more by what they value. People who are more Perceiving tend to want to put off making decisions until they have enough information to feel comfortable, while people who prefer Judging will push more quickly to make a decision.

Since none of these variables are in themselves right or wrong there are no right or wrong types, yet the descriptions enable people to see how they differ from others, and how they may be like others in particular ways. The MBTI describes preferences in how people use their energy, how they collect information, how they use information, and how they make decisions. Using the MBTI allows individuals in a workshop to appreciate both themselves and the unique gifts of others. For example, one principal now provides questions for his leadership team ahead of time, so that Introverts, who tend to "think to talk" as described in the MBTI, will participate more during the meeting.

Our purpose in using the MBTI in SDP is to foster an understanding and appreciation of both ourselves and others so that we are more likely to act in no-fault ways. As we learn about and accept ourselves, we are able to move beyond our type. As we learn about and accept others, we are able to help them move beyond their type. Although probably not possible in a lifetime, the ideal of the fully developed person is one who has developed all of the preferences of each of the 16 personality types.

Figure 12.4 The Myers-Briggs Type Indicator® (MBTI®) short descriptions

THOROUGH (ISTJ) Success earned. Will concentrate and are thorough. Serious and quiet. See to it everything is organized.	RESPONSIBLE (ISFJ) Quiet, friendly, responsible, and conscientious. Thorough, painstaking, and accurate.	PERSEVERE (INFJ) Succeed by perseverance, originality, and desire to do whatever is needed or wanted.	ORIGINAL MINDS (INTJ) Usually have original minds and great drive for their own ideas and purposes. Independent and determined.
ANALYZE LIFE (ISTP) Cool onlookers—quiet, reserved, observing and analyzing life with detached curiosity. Look at cause and effect.	LOYAL FOLLOWERS (ISFP) Relaxed, retiring, friendly, sensitive, and kind. Modest about their abilities. Do not force their opinions or values on others.	HELPERS (INFP) Full of enthusiasms and loyalties but seldom talk of these until they know you well. Ready to help anyone with a problem.	LOGICAL (INTP) Quiet, reserved, impersonal, and logical. Can argue either side of an issue. Interested in ideas. Have sharply defined interests.
MATTER OF FACT (ESTP) Tend to be mechanical. Do not worry. Enjoy whatever comes along. Tend to like taking things apart and putting them back together.	COMMON SENSE (ESFP) Outgoing, easygoing, accepting, and friendly. Enjoy everything. Best at common sense and practical ability.	ENTHUSIASTIC (ENFP) Warm, high-spirited, ingenious, and imaginative. Quick with solutions. Ability to improvise.	RESOURCEFUL (ENTP) Quick, alert, outspoken. One new interest after another. Quick, ingenious, and resourceful in solving new and challenging problems.
ORGANIZE AND ADMINISTRATE (ESTJ) Practical and realistic. Like to organize and run activities.	COOPERATORS (ESFJ) Warm-hearted. Talkative and born cooperators. Like harmony. Active committee members.	RESPONSIVE (ENFJ) Social, responsible, and sympathetic. Feel real concern for what others think and want.	DECISIVE LEADERS (ENTJ) Hearty and frank. Good at anything requiring reasoning. Usually well informed.

The Enneagram

Ennea in Greek is *nine;* the Enneagram describes nine personality types (see Figure 12.5). For convenience, I have listed the nine personality types as a square, although the Enneagram is usually depicted as a circle, showing how the nine personalities connect to one another.

The Enneagram is an oral tradition that has been passed down through many centuries, and its exact origin is not known. Only recently have people begun to describe in writing the nine personalities that are a part of the Enneagram. The focus of the model, unlike the MBTI, has been on helping people discover the primary fixation (addiction, fault, negative, defensive trait) of their personality type. Studying each of the nine personality types in depth supports the development of self-knowledge and wisdom and the eventual discovery of where one fits on the chart (the "gram"). Each

Figure 12.5 The Enneagram

1 **Perfectionist** I want to be perfect. Use high standards to point out how to improve.	2 **Helper** I want to be caring. Pay attention to what others want and need.	3 **Motivator** I want to be successful. Set goals and strive for accomplishments.
4 **Individualist** I want to be unique. See many sides to a situation.	5 **Observer** I want to be all knowing. Study situations with a detached point of view.	6 **Questioner** I want to see what could go wrong. Question and analyze situations.
7 **Adventurer** I want to experience everything. Put focus on future possibilities.	8 **Boss** I want to be powerful. Take action to make things happen.	9 **Peacemaker** I want to be content. Work to resolve conflicts by listening and accommodating others.

personality is assigned a number. For example, if you ascertain that you are a "1" on the Enneagram, your negative trait is said to be "perfection." What that means, briefly, is that unconsciously you frequently overwork yourself to achieve perfection in order to hide your insecurities.

The Enneagram enables people to do more in-depth self-reflection and to free themselves from their negative traits. In interpersonal relationships, it helps us to accept that everyone, including ourselves, has deficiencies. The Enneagram provides a way to understand and accept this fact. It also gives specific suggestions for how people can develop.

Archetypes

The Archetype model is a description of 12 energies or patterns (see Figure 12.6). Unlike the first two models, however, the Archetype model is based on the notion that all of the archetypes exist in everyone and are available to them. They are patterns that are found throughout time and in all cultures. Because of upbringing, training, experiences in life, or present situations, certain archetypes emerge in the moment and drive behavior. Because each of these energies or patterns can take a positive or negative form, the archetypal pattern has the potential to "grab hold of us" and make us act in ways that we do not intend.

An example of Archetypes in action might be the parent who comes into a classroom after school and shouts at the teacher for "being unfair" to a child. In archetypal language this would demonstrate the tendency of that parent to react with the strong negative archetypal energy of the Warrior. A natural reaction of the teacher would be to become defensive by being critical of the parent—in effect, tapping into the teacher's own negative archetypal energy of the Warrior.

Figure 12.6 Archetypes: Short descriptions of patterns of energy within us

Innocent	Seeker	Ruler
Trusts others and creates trust. Is open and willing to try new things. Is idealistic and optimistic.	Searches for opportunities. Ventures into the unknown. Is curious and inquisitive. Explores new ideas.	Organizes and structures activities for self and others. Takes responsibility and provides stability.
Orphan/ Empathizer	**Destroyer/Judge/Liberator**	**Magician**
Knows and relates to how others feel because of having had the experience of how difficult life can be.	Ends old ways to make way for the new. Can make hard decisions by facing reality and prioritizing.	Intuitively knows what, when, and how to change. Can transform others through use of energy. Heals others. Demonstrates win/ win possibilities.
Warrior	**Lover/Motivator**	**Sage**
Challenges wrongs. Fights for a cause or to accomplish own goals. Has strength of conviction.	Has passion for a cause, people, ideas, LIFE. Dedication leads to making strong commitments.	Reflects using a global perspective. Uses own experiences and knowledge to see patterns and to guide others.
Caregiver	**Creator**	**Jester**
Reaches out to others and provides help and support. Nurtures, guides, and serves others.	Thinks "outside the box." Is innovative and inspired. Looks for the unusual. Solves problems by having a different perspective.	Enjoys life. Is uninhibited. Plays and has fun. Does not take self or others too seriously.

SOURCE: Adapted in part from Carol S. Pearson's concept of twelve archetypes. For more information, see *Awakening the Heroes Within: Twelve Archetypes to Help Us Find Ourselves and Transform Our World*, New York: HarperCollins, 1991. Copyright © 1991 by Carol S. Pearson.

By becoming aware of his or her probable response, the teacher could choose to act from another, positive archetypal energy and change the whole tone of the interaction. If, for example, the teacher responds as a Caregiver and says, "Oh, I am sorry, I was just trying to help when I told your child that she had to study harder. She felt so badly the last time she took the test and received a poor grade." Or the Ruler might say, "I want every child to succeed so I make sure I tell every child they have to work hard. I would not want to single your child out." A positive Orphan response might be, "I feel bad if your child was hurt or embarrassed by what I said. I will talk to her tomorrow so that she feels better." The point of this is that we do not have to just react to what comes up in us first. Humans are complex; we can tap into other parts of ourselves that are just as authentic and yet at the same time may be more appropriate and constructive.

The Archetypes are similar to subpersonalities that emerge, as needed, to help achieve goals. But, because they are unconsciously learned, they may drive people to act in ways that are not appropriate to a particular situation. People may ignore a certain archetypal pattern, or only see, experience, or act from the negative side of the archetype. The value in using this model is that it helps individuals to become aware "in the moment," and to change their responses in ways that can be more helpful to them and to others.

As I said earlier, this is meant to be a very short course in understanding people. It is most helpful when adults commit themselves to developing over the course of their lives. However, just knowing this much may help people to be more patient, more accepting of differences in others, and less fault finding. In fact, people may begin to see that the very uniqueness of each human being contributes to the richness of everyone in the school community.

REFERENCES

Berne, E. (1964). *Games people play: The psychology of human relationships.* New York: Grove.

Horney, K. (1950). *Neurosis and human growth: The struggle toward self-realization.* New York: Norton.

Luft, J., & Ingham, H. (1963). *Group processes: An introduction to group dynamics.* Palo Alto, CA: National Press Books.

Myers, I. B. (1998). *Introduction to type: A guide to understanding your results on the Myers-Briggs Type Indicator.* Palo Alto, CA: Consulting Psychologist Press.

Myers, I. B. with Myers (1995). *Gifts differing: Understanding personality type.* Palo Alto, CA: CPP, Inc. Modified and reproduced by special permission of the Publisher, Davies Black Publishing, an imprint of CPP, Inc., Palo Alto, CA 94303. Copyright 1995 by Davies Black Publishing, an imprint of CPP, Inc. All rights reserved. Further reproduction is prohibited without the Publisher's written consent.

Pearson, C. S. (1991). *Awakening the heroes within: Twelve archetypes to help us find ourselves and transform our world.* San Francisco: HarperSanFrancisco.

Rogers, C. R. (1980). *A way of being.* Boston: Houghton Mifflin.

FURTHER READING

Palmer, H. (1988). *The Enneagram: Understanding yourself and others in your life.* New York: HarperCollins.

Riso, D. R., & Hudson, R. (1999). *The wisdom of the Enneagram.* New York: Bantam Books.

READ MORE ABOUT . . .

For a full description of the framework of the container, see Chapter 10 in this volume, "A Team Approach to Educational Change."

For more information on feedback, see the section titled "Feedback Description Guides" in Chapter 10 in this volume, "A Team Approach to Educational Change."

13

Three Guiding Principles for Interactions on Teams

J. Patrick Howley

It's one thing to know about the guiding principles of no-fault, consensus, and collaboration; it's another thing to live and work by them. SDP's director of Teaching and Adult Development offers real-world insights into applying these foundational concepts to everyday life in schools.

The three guiding principles of the Comer Process are no-fault, consensus, and collaboration. Acting as boundaries, they help teams to stop to think about their behaviors so that, as Dr. Comer has said, members "don't victimize others with their own shortcomings." When teams live faithfully by these principles, they spend less energy on adult issues and focus more on children.

Teams become stronger when they have a clear and common understanding of what is meant by no-fault, consensus, and collaboration. Therefore the School Development Program (SDP) encourages teams to engage in discussions regarding what is meant by the guiding principles, and what it means to follow them in school and on teams.

No-fault simply means that we do not blame others for a failure or mistake but, instead, use our energy to define and solve the problem. We start with no-fault because Dr. Comer believes that without first using that guiding principle we will be unable to do any other work effectively. If teams are busy blaming others, they have focused their energy away from finding solutions. Teams that operate under this principle focus first on *what* went wrong and not on *who* did wrong. They discuss how to correct the problem, and then focus on how they can prevent it from happening again.

Consensus means that members on teams, after much discussion and dialogue, come to a general or common agreement. Members agree to make and support a decision for an action step even if they do not fully agree with it. This can occur only if each member's voice has been heard and reflected on by the team. Team members also agree to review the decision after a period of time in order to revise it if necessary.

Collaboration means working together. People who collaborate support one another in both joint and individual efforts. For example, teachers share lesson plans that have worked for them. They get together to design a unit. In teams that collaborate, members meet, share ideas, and after meetings, take responsibility for following through with individual action steps. Their individual efforts are then brought back to the team so that everyone's actions become part of an integrated and coordinated effort. Everyone commits to communicating and supporting one another and as a result, experiences a sense of community in doing their work.

Each of these concepts at first seems simple. Yet when they are discussed in more depth, teams begin to understand and appreciate their complexity, and how easily they can be misunderstood. It is helpful, therefore, to elaborate on each of these guiding principles.

NO-FAULT PROBLEM SOLVING

There is a tendency in human nature to look outward and make judgments of others. There is also a tendency not to look inward to see the changes that we ourselves might need to make. No-fault helps members adjust these natural human tendencies to focus on the tasks the team is trying to accomplish. No-fault encourages people to consider the premise that other people's mistakes result from misunderstandings and miscommunications and not from a deliberate attempt to offend or do poor work. People live the no-fault principle when they *consciously* decide to make the assumption that others have good intentions, and check with team members about their intentions before they rush to judgment.

A safe environment is created when a team operates on the principle of no-fault. That safety enables people to take risks by directly sharing their thoughts and feelings. It frees people to work without fear. Everyone makes mistakes. When team members allow for mistakes, they are better able to learn and grow from them. An example is the invention process. Any inventor is braving the unknown, and that takes tremendous courage. It also takes a high tolerance for failure, determination, and the perseverance to endure. The Wright brothers, for example, crashed their plane countless times before they were successful. They had to constantly reassess, study, tinker, and modify before finding the right solution to achieving flight.

Solving problems in schools often requires creative solutions. Initially, some attempts at problem solving will fail. Problem solving is a form of learning. Schools are learning organizations, not only for children, but also for adults. Learning is sometimes a humbling activity because learners are venturing into the unknown.

No one wants to fail—especially in front of others. When following the principle of no-fault, a climate of trust balances the risk of the venture.

Our expectation of no-fault means that teams will focus on their work with children, not on what is wrong with people. No-fault does not equate to no accountability. Think of the government task force that probes into the causes of space shuttle disasters. It investigates every possibility of what went wrong, and why it went wrong, in order to prevent future disasters. It is not conducted as a witch hunt, but as a probe into what may have been overlooked or taken for granted. The task force has learned through experience that everyone makes mistakes. Therefore it has to check its own work again and again. The task force understands that it is human to make mistakes, and it must, where lives are in danger, take that fact into account.

No-fault does not mean that team members withhold their honest thoughts and feelings from the individuals who provoked them. Members learn, however, to share their thoughts and feelings in a manner that does not diminish or demean another person. That is why we make a point of helping people learn the skill of giving non-judgmental feedback.

At SDP, we believe that no-fault is directly related to problem solving. When a no-fault approach is used in problem solving, everyone shares equal responsibility for failures as well as successes. Rather than point fingers of blame, individuals seek to identify causes of problems and address them. As a result, personal development and the development of the team become primary values. By valuing development (growth, change, learning), members provide information (feedback) to the team, which helps everyone improve.

Again, no-fault does not mean no accountability. It means *everyone* becomes accountable. Accountability thus becomes a team or group responsibility, and each individual contributes to the work of the group. The team's energy is unleashed on solving problems and implementing solutions, rather than being diverted into personal and judgmental faultfinding.

CONSENSUS DECISION MAKING

Making decisions by consensus prevents the perception that there are winners and losers. SDP does value *what* we accomplish. We also value *how* we accomplish it. What consensus provides is a structure that opens up the process of discussion and dialogue to ensure that the *quality* of each decision is addressed. The primary barrier to reaching consensus is the time it takes. The value, however, is that it opens up the process to include all the stakeholders so that more data are collected and discussed. This enables teams to make higher quality decisions. Consensus also challenges people to put themselves in the place of others. In consensus we find ways to bring diverse voices together to work for the betterment of children.

Consensus means a general agreement. Therefore consensus does not mean *everyone* has to agree with a decision. An issue does not have to be tabled if everyone does not agree. The decision does not need to be modified to the satisfaction of *every* team member. These actions would completely paralyze a team. What it does mean is that *every voice is heard*. This is important for two reasons. First, as alternative opinions and the rationales for the decisions are discussed, the team acquires more data regarding the decision. The process is slower than voting. Going slowly fosters higher quality decision making. Second, because their opinions have been listened to and respected by the team, members are more likely to feel a sense of ownership in the decision even if that decision is not the one they were advocating.

Consensus puts the focus on listening more than on talking. Much listening needs to take place. Consensus cannot be reached until we hear from all team members and until team members have heard from members of the school community. Consensus involves brainstorming, extensive discussion and dialogue, and identification and prioritization of issues and possible solutions. A team can move to consensus when the chairperson, facilitator, or principal says, "It seems as if we are pretty much in agreement on this. Is that right?" If people disagree, they can then say why they disagree. When the team actively listens and encourages people to voice their differences and their reasons for having those differences, people are more likely to be able to "let go" and support a decision even if they disagree with it. The result of making decisions by consensus is that everyone feels a part of the process and can therefore claim a stake in the activities and decisions made by the school.

By way of example, one school's School Planning and Management Team (SPMT) gave everyone in the community a voice to influence future decisions of their team by creating four three-by-five index cards that asked: (1) "What do you see as the major strengths of this school?" (2) "What do you see as major weaknesses of this school?" (3) "What changes or improvements would you like to see in the school?" (4) "Would you like to have a role in helping the school improve? If so, please put your name and number on the card." At the faculty meeting teachers filled out the cards, discussed them in grade-level groups, and reported out; then they handed in their cards to members of the SPMT. The SPMT members had a table set up at the entrance of the school on teacher conference night. They asked parents to fill out the cards while they were waiting for their conference and then hand them to an SPMT member (designated by a red name tag), or simply put them back on the front table. The SPMT analyzed these data and used the information throughout the year to guide and focus their decision-making process.

Teams need to learn to be more comfortable with this less structured and more divergent process because consensus implies that teams will explore issues in more depth. Rather than meetings becoming debates in which members' first response is, "I disagree. I think we should . . . ," they become conversations in which the first response is, "I never thought of looking at it like that. Tell me more about your thinking. How did it bring you to that conclusion?" The main challenge in reaching consensus is the ability of team members to temporarily put aside their own point of view so they can understand the points of view of others. Through a process of dialogue rather than just discussion, teams learn to think together and to come to a common understanding on the important issues they are addressing. Edgar Schein (1984) described consensus this way:

> I understand what most of you would like to do. I personally would not do that, but I feel that you understand what my alternative would be. I have had sufficient opportunity to sway you to my point of view but clearly have not been able to do so. Therefore, I will gladly go along with what most of you wish to do. (p. 56)

Consensus strengthens our problem solving by moving us away from issues of personal power and toward the group power of helping others, namely, children.

This process implies that when adults have a common understanding and knowledge of what constitutes effective child development, it will be much easier for them to come to consensus.

Consensus decision making requires that team members

- share data collected regarding an issue

- openly discuss their own position on an issue

- demonstrate that they understand each other's positions

- commit to supporting the group's general agreement on their final decision, even if they do not completely agree with it

- revisit a decision to see if it is working, discuss any new data collected, and modify or change the decision, if necessary

Ed Joyner, executive director of SDP, has said, "Consensus allows us to pursue the most practical course and to change to other choices when the first choice is insufficient."

Teachers and parents need to understand that not every decision a school makes should be made by consensus. This would completely paralyze the principal and the school system. Teachers and parents need to understand that it is usually the principal who is ultimately held accountable. In fact, the number of decisions made by consensus within the school may be small. These may, however, be the school's most important decisions. Generally, decisions that will directly impact the development of children (any of the six developmental pathways) are made by the SPMT using the consensus process. Decisions that need to be made quickly and that are a matter of the general running of the building operations are usually made by the principal, sometimes with little input or discussion from staff or the SPMT. Decisions that are mandated by law, district goals, or state mandates are expedited by the principal. To avoid confusion, some schools and districts have discussed and even listed areas of decision making are within in the domain of the principal and areas that are within the domain of the SPMT.

COLLABORATIVE RELATIONSHIPS

One hot summer day, I rushed into an electronics store in central Connecticut to buy a gift for my wife while my aging mother was grocery shopping next door. I had already visited the electronics store twice so I knew exactly what I wanted to purchase. I wanted to buy it as fast as I could so I could get back to help my mother shop. I purchased it rather quickly, but then had to wait for a very long time for someone to get the box from the storeroom in the back. I watched as seven men who worked in the store stood around not doing much of anything while one man, tired and sweaty, went running back and forth to fulfill the orders. Finally I asked, "Why can't one of those men help me?" "Oh," the cashier exclaimed, "that's not their job. They are salesmen." That is not an example of collaboration. If the store wanted to serve its customers better, those men would have taken their jackets off and pitched in to help an overworked employee. Let me repeat, that was an example of exactly what collaboration is not!

Not long after that, my wife and I visited a small coffee shop that we like to go to for Saturday morning breakfast. It was so crowded on this particular day that we sat at the counter. What a show we observed! One waitress started to make coffee but then hurried over to wait on a customer who wanted to pay his bill. Meanwhile, another waiter came by and saw the coffee almost ready to be put in the machine, and he finished the job. The waitress came back and then yelled out, "Thanks, whoever helped me with the coffee!" Someone put bread in the conveyer toaster, and as it popped out someone else came and buttered it, and still another waitress put the toast in front of us. "Now that is collaboration!" I said to my wife.

Of course, in schools a collaborative process is much more difficult to create. The differences in experience, perceptions, ways of thinking, and levels of development tend to cause fragmentation in schools. Fragmentation, therefore, becomes the primary challenge to building collaborative relationships.

Collaboration on teams requires mutual respect. It also requires a true partnership in which teachers, support staff, the administrative team, and parents build trusting and supportive relationships. Traditional schools operate exclusively in a hierarchy of relationships with the people at the top having all or most of the power. At SDP, we honor both top-down and bottom-up decision making. This means that (1) we recognize that certain positions of leadership and responsibility give principals and the central office the right to make final decisions, and (2) the voices of the school community are heard by the leaders when open and trusting relationships are fostered. As a result there is both top-down and bottom-up support for the essence of SDP. The bottom-up aspect suggests that students, parents, and school staff believe in the process, claim ownership of it, and support it. As applied to teams, a commitment to collaboration results in a climate of cooperation, trust, and support. The challenge for a principal is to avoid using the team as a rubber stamp. The challenge for members of the team is to avoid paralyzing the team by focusing on adult issues. A former SDP staff member, Jack Gillette, used to say, "Collaboration means working with the enemy." Initially, we may see others who disagree with us as the enemy. In fact, part of the challenge in collaboration is learning to see that others are not the enemy, but are people who see the world differently. We have found that sometimes you have the most to learn from that "enemy."

Thinking territorially creates enemies. Thinking collaboratively creates a mindset of, "We are all in this together. If you lose, I lose. If you win, I win."

Collaboration implies that people on teams are interdependent. The principal needs the teachers and so agrees to be responsive to all of them. The teachers need the principal, who has the legal responsibility in the school, and so they agree to not block his or her efforts. In order to succeed with children, we need one another. The school needs to hear from parents in order to know what children are experiencing at home. The parents also need to hear from teachers in order to know how children are engaged during the day in the classroom. In addition, we need to hear from support staff and ancillary services so that we know what happens to children not only in the classroom, but also in other parts of the school.

Because school life mirrors society in being so complex, collaboration ensures deeper and richer communication among all the adults who interact with children. When we as adults talk with one another about children, we gain a more global perspective about child development. A global perspective leads to more thoughtful interventions. Collaboration provides a means to understand, coordinate, and integrate fragmented efforts to improve a school. The principal has the primary role in creating collaborative relationships. By being willing to be inclusive, invitational, open, and nonauthoritarian; by allowing people to make choices; and by encouraging people to speak their own mind, the principal facilitates the growth and development of leadership throughout the school.

THE CHALLENGES OF WORKING WITH THE THREE GUIDING PRINCIPLES

When I first came to work at SDP, one of the staff members commented that the components of SDP had challenged her and helped her to grow personally as well as professionally. Some time later, when our research was showing that, of the nine elements of the Comer Process, no-fault was the most difficult to implement, I began to think more about how each of the three guiding principles was a challenge to me personally. I asked myself, "When do I have the most difficulty with the three guiding principles?" This is what came from that thinking:

I have difficulty with no-fault

. . . when I don't feel appreciated and I need the appreciation.
. . . when I don't feel listened to.
. . . when I or others put unrealistic expectations on me.
. . . when others seem or are judgmental.
. . . when I am under pressure from a tight deadline.
. . . when I don't feel respected.
. . . when I am embarrassed publicly.

I have difficulty with consensus

. . . when I want control over a situation.
. . . when I want more power to change something.
. . . when I feel the pressure of time.
. . . when I feel others are trying to take control.
. . . when I feel others are being manipulative.
. . . when I don't trust the people or the process.

I have difficulty with collaboration

. . . when I don't know the people I am working with.
. . . when I don't trust the people I am working with.
. . . when I feel the pressure of time.
. . . when I don't feel others are collaborating with me.
. . . when I want power and/or control.

REFERENCE

Schein, E. (1984). *Process consultation: Its role in organization development.* Reading, MA: Addison-Wesley.

READ MORE ABOUT . . .

For information on no-fault and accountability, see M. Ben-Avie, A. Sanford, L. Young, S. Evans-Tranumn, C. Grant, E. Vega, E. Joyner, & T. R. Steinfeld (1999). No-fault and accountability. In J. P. Comer, M. Ben-Avie, N. M. Haynes, & E. T. Joyner, *Child by child* (pp. 7-24). New York: Teachers College Press.

Part III

A Time to Act

Edward T. Joyner

The first part of this volume, Chapters 1–8, presented the idea of child and adolescent development as the foundation of education. The second part, Chapters 9–13, was devoted to adult development. The take-home message is that to help students succeed with multiple options, we cannot ignore our own development. The concluding part of this volume is structured in two sections. In these two sections, we answer a question posed to us by a reporter: "What do you mean by child and adolescent development as the foundation of education—aren't teachers required to take a college course on child development?" We begin answering this question by presenting research on children and trauma, and research on children during wartime. Some children are born in very hard places. SDP's message is that "child development" is not a college course—it is a call to action. It is a call to action that encompasses the whole community. When the lifepaths of children are at stake, we cannot remain idle.

SDP school communities have responded to the call. The volume concludes with the narrative about Fienberg/Fisher Elementary School. This school is one of the most deprived and neglected schools in the area of South Beach in Miami, Florida. The school serves poor immigrant families from all over the globe, many of them refugees from countries at war. Grace Nebb, the principal, shows how the community activated itself to promote the students' learning and development. The outcome? The Florida Accountability System awarded the school a grade of "A." Through its transformation the school now provides stability and hope for current and future students.

14

Children and Trauma

Robert A. Murphy

One of SDP's special qualities is its insistence on providing support for all students and their families along all developmental pathways. Students who have experienced war-related and other types of physical and emotional trauma have urgent psychological needs that are often misdiagnosed as learning disabilities. Meeting these needs can be a complex undertaking that involves the entire school community. The research coordinator of the Yale Child Study Center's National Center for Children Exposed to Violence offers an introduction to the subject that can be used as (1) a solid argument to support requests for in-depth staff development on these subjects, and (2) a primer in recognizing often misdiagnosed behaviors as indicators of acute or chronic trauma.

Exposure to trauma, such as violence, injury, death, warfare, and disaster, among other circumstances, disrupts the basic preconditions for optimal child development. In the face of overwhelming circumstances children are unable to contain and cope with their thoughts, emotions, and behaviors. The disruption of psychological and biological systems may lead to symptoms of physical arousal, withdrawal, and reexperiencing of traumatic events; other children may develop specific, circumscribed symptoms such as disruptions in sleeping, eating, and toileting (Boney-McCoy & Finkelhor, 1996; Foy & Goguen, 1998; Gorman-Smith & Tolan, 1998).

As a result of exposure to trauma, children can become distracted, unable to concentrate or pay attention in school or at home. Chronic exposure to trauma is

Table 14.1   Children's responses to traumatic events

Type of Reaction	Types of Symptoms
Emotional	Irritability, aggressive behavior, angry outbursts, tantrums, difficulty being soothed, tearfulness, sadness, anxiety, fearfulness
Cognitive	Difficulty concentrating, inattention, daydreaming, forgetting aspects of the trauma
Reexperiencing the trauma	Preoccupation with frightening thoughts and feelings, risk taking, repetitive play related to the trauma
Loss of developmental skills	Loss of previously attained developmental skills, acting immature or "babyish"
Physical arousal	Feeling on guard, more easily startled, sensitivity and upset in response to traumatic cues or reminders (e.g., images, feelings), changeability in mood and behavior
Separation anxiety	School refusal, difficulty with separations, complaints of loneliness, increased neediness with caregivers
Sleep problems	Nightmares, difficulty falling asleep, waking during the night, enuresis
Physical complaints	Headaches, stomachaches, aches and pains without medical etiology
Social withdrawal	Loss of interest (e.g., in peers, school, or pleasurable activities), social isolation, emotional numbing, avoidance of traumatic cues or reminders

associated with increased depression and anxiety, alcohol use, and lower school achievement (Pfefferbaum, 1997; Widom, 1999). Other long-term adaptations to trauma can involve an increased likelihood of victimization, as well as the perpetration of violence. In those impoverished areas where the prevalence of violence is especially high, there may be a progression from witnessing to being the victim of and then to engaging in violence. An overview of children's responses to traumatic events is presented in Table 14.1.

Children and families who are most vulnerable to the effects of trauma may also lack sufficient mental health care. Those who simultaneously contend with the effects of trauma, poverty, social adversity, and preexisting mental health problems may be unable to make use of traditional clinic- or office-based services when they are available. In essence, those with the greatest need may receive the least care. In response to these concerns, there has been a proliferation of community-based services through which health care is provided in schools, homes, and community settings, with an emphasis on engaging with and stabilizing families in distress, and collaborating with other community providers

(Comer, Ben-Avie, Haynes, & Joyner, 1999; Marans, Murphy, & Berkowitz, 2002; Murphy, 2002).

TRAUMA'S IMPACT ON CHILD DEVELOPMENT

Developmental status becomes especially important in understanding how a specific child may respond to traumatic experiences (Berkowitz & Murphy, 2000; Pynoos, Steinberg, & Wraith, 1995). Infants and very young children are unable to express their reactions to traumatic and violent events through words. Instead, their responses will be evident in changes in their behavior and regression to earlier developmental levels. An infant who is typically well modulated and easily soothed may become cranky, appear colicky, refuse food, and be difficult to soothe. Although a child's relationship and contact with his or her primary caregiver remains crucial at all stages of development, separations are particularly difficult for infants. Infants cannot consider the future or the possibility of reunion with a loved one and are much more dependent on the physical presence of the caregiver than are older children.

Toddlers rely on their primary caregiver, who—ideally—provides a secure base for exploring the world and is a consistent, reliable, and emotionally available person. With increased physical abilities, cognitive capacities, and language development, children strive for feelings of mastery and competence, which can be undermined by feeling small and helpless, as occurs during a traumatic event. Toddlers may present with a range of symptoms, including anxiety, clinginess, inconsolability, sleep disturbances, toileting problems, and temper tantrums.

Imaginative play becomes a central means for preschool children to express feelings and ideas about themselves and the world, and the development of language and symbolic play contributes to enhanced abilities to cope with stress or trauma. Nevertheless, preschoolers may become agitated, and—despite having already passed appropriate developmental milestones—they may regress to less mature modes of coping (e.g., nightmares, temper tantrums, and irritability).

Younger children's concrete thinking and reasoning complicates helping them cope with the effects of trauma. Abstract events and concepts such as "death," "heaven," and "God" are confusing and easily misconstrued. A child attempting to make sense of fragmentary knowledge and frightening memories may generate personal "explanations" that can be scarier or more distressing than what actually occurred. With their egocentric style of thinking, young children may inaccurately assume that their thoughts and feelings were the cause of traumatic events around them.

During elementary school years, children become involved in social activities with friends, participating in sports and school activities. Principles of fairness and rules govern their actions and determine their judgments about their own actions and those of others. School-aged children are better equipped to cope with trauma and violence due to their development in the use of thought and language to regulate behavior and express complex ideas.

School-aged children may respond to trauma with circumscribed symptoms. Their academic and social performance may falter, or they may engage in behaviors that cause distress to those around them, such as lying, stealing, or fighting. Sleep and eating may be disturbed due to underlying thoughts and distressing feelings. In response to trauma, school-aged children may battle parents for control in one or more areas related to food, hygiene, or household responsibilities. Finally, school-aged children may respond with excitement or awe over the magnitude of violence or the technological power of weapons and their effects.

Adolescents may worry about the potential loss of adult help and protection alongside their wish to be independent of adult authority and control. They may engage in hostile, aggressive, or risk-taking behavior in an effort to ward off feelings of vulnerability and to save face, particularly in the presence of peers. Adolescents also can harness their increasing cognitive and physical capacities to engage in self-protective behavior in the face of trauma. They can use positive relationships with adults to cope more effectively, yet their urgent wish to appear strong and adult-like leaves them prone to feelings of guilt and inadequacy when they are confronted by overwhelming situations. Adolescents who are unable to adapt successfully following trauma may experience chronic difficulties in school (including truancy and dropping out), in their peer and family relationships, and at work; some may engage in high-risk behaviors related to sexual activity and substance abuse.

POSTTRAUMATIC SYMPTOMS

Children's reactions to trauma can be divided into three aspects: traumatic exposure, traumatic reminders, and secondary stress (Pynoos et al., 1995). Traumatic exposure includes characteristics of the traumatic or violent event. Traumatic reminders or cues evoke the initial traumatic experience and may increase posttraumatic responses. Children who contend with secondary stress in the form of preexisting psychiatric problems, family disturbance, and psychosocial adversity may fare least well in response to the additional pressure of a new trauma.

A range of factors influences the extent to which children develop posttraumatic symptoms. Exposure to a single traumatic event is more strongly related to the development of traditional posttraumatic stress disorder (PTSD) symptoms such as intrusive thoughts, hypersensitivity, and anxiety, while exposure to multiple traumas is more strongly connected to enduring changes in mood, behavior, and social functioning. Intentional trauma, especially when inflicted by a loved one, may result in greater damage to a child's sense of trust and security, as the child must contend with not only the sequelae of the actual trauma but also the loss of a secure and benevolent relationship. Physical proximity to a traumatic event, whether as a victim or a witness, increases the likelihood of psychological impairment, while greater physical distance may attenuate the reaction. Similarly, greater traumatization will likely accompany events that are life threatening or extremely violent. Psychological proximity may affect responses in a similar manner, so that exposure to violence inflicted on a loved one will be more disruptive than witnessing violence perpetrated against a stranger.

Children react to trauma in ways that can be partially predicted by their gender. Boys tend to express their distress in the form of externalizing symptoms. They may become oppositional, aggressive, impulsive, defiant, hyperactive, or inattentive. In

CHILDREN AND TRAUMA **163**

contrast, girls tend to present with internalizing symptoms of depression, anxiety, or physical complaints.

Statistics show that African American and Hispanic youth are more likely to be exposed to violence and other traumatic events, but these differences appear to reflect differences in socioeconomic status (Gorman-Smith & Tolan, 1998; Hurt, Malmud, Brodsky, & Gianetta, 2001; Schwab-Stone et al., 1999). Thus higher rates of posttraumatic symptoms are attributable to socioeconomic disadvantage, which can affect levels of family stress, neighborhood safety, and individual coping skills, as well as access to quality medical and mental health care.

PARENTS AND CAREGIVERS

Parents and other adult caregivers perform a crucial role in determining how children will respond to traumatic events. In the best circumstances, parents assist children to express and manage their thoughts and feelings. Alternatively, when parents themselves become symptomatic, they may be less available to their children and more limited in their ability to consider the effects of traumatic exposure on their children's functioning. When parents are directly involved as victims or perpetrators, children may have the greatest difficulty. The resultant parental unavailability is compounded by the rupture of the relationship brought about by seeing parents involved in a violent or traumatic altercation. In contrast, the presence of a stable and psychologically available primary caregiver in the home moderates the extent to which children will be negatively affected by exposure to violence and trauma in their communities and neighborhoods.

MENTAL HEALTH PROVIDERS

Mental health providers also play a crucial role in ameliorating the effects of children's exposure to trauma. Some children may benefit from short-term interventions focused on the trauma and their subsequent reactions, while others, particularly those with lives marked by extended periods of adversity, are more likely to require approaches that address both the difficulties related to the trauma and preexisting problems related to individual, family, and school functioning (Pfefferbaum, 2002).

SCHOOL-BASED INTERVENTIONS

Children may falter in their school performance due to intrusive thoughts and lapses in concentration due to their preoccupation with memories and reminders of a traumatic experience. School-based interventions for children affected by trauma represent a useful adjunct to traditional treatment approaches as they foster greater competence among educators in responding to children's problems (Newgass & Schonfeld, 2000) and provide children with a context in which to express their concerns related to trauma and grief among like-minded peers (Saltzman, Steinberg, Layne, Aisenberg, & Pynoos, 2001).

REFERENCES

Berkowitz, S. J., & Murphy, R. A. (2000). Child development and education. In N. S. S. Center (Ed.), *COPS in schools: SRO training curriculum*. Westlake Village, CA: National School Safety Center.

Boney-McCoy, S., & Finkelhor, D. (1996). Is youth victimization related to trauma symptoms and depression after controlling for prior symptoms and family relationships? A longitudinal, prospective study. *Journal of Consulting and Clinical Psychology, 64,* 1406–1416.

Comer, J. P., Ben-Avie, M., Haynes, N. M., & Joyner, E. T. (Eds.). (1999). *Child by child: The Comer process for change in education*. New York: Teachers College Press.

Foy, D. W., & Goguen, C. A. (1998). Community violence-related PTSD in children and adolescents. *PTSD Research Quarterly, 9,* 1–6.

Gorman-Smith, D., & Tolan, P. (1998). The role of exposure to community violence and developmental problems among inner-city youth. *Development and Psychopathology, 10,* 101–116.

Hurt, H., Malmud, E., Brodsky, N. L., & Gianetta, J. (2001). Exposure to violence: Psychological and academic correlates in child witnesses. *Archives of Pediatric and Adolescent Medicine, 155,* 1351–1356.

Marans, S., Murphy, R. A., & Berkowitz, S. J. (2002). Police-mental health responses to children exposed to violence: The Child Development Community Policing Program. In M. Lewis (Ed.), *Comprehensive textbook of child and adolescent psychiatry*. Baltimore, MD: Williams & Wilkins.

Murphy, R. A. (2002). Mental health, juvenile justice, and law enforcement responses to youth psychopathology. In D. T. Marsh & M. A. Fristad (Eds.), *Handbook of serious emotional disturbance in children and adolescents*. New York: John Wiley.

Newgass, S., & Schonfeld, D. J. (2000). School crisis intervention, crisis prevention, and crisis response. In A. R. Roberts (Ed.), *Crisis intervention handbook: Assessment, treatment, and research* (pp. 209–228). New York: Oxford University Press.

Pfefferbaum, B. (1997). Posttraumatic stress disorder in children: A review of the past 10 years. *Journal of the American Academy of Child and Adolescent Psychiatry, 36,* 1503–1511.

Pfefferbaum, B. (2002). Posttraumatic stress disorder. In M. Lewis (Ed.), *Child and adolescent psychiatry: A comprehensive textbook* (3rd ed., pp. 912–925). Philadelphia: Lippincott Williams & Wilkins.

Pynoos, R. S., Steinberg, A. M., & Wraith, R. (1995). A developmental model of childhood traumatic stress. In D. Cicchetti & D. J. Cohen (Eds.), *Developmental psychopathology: Vol. 2. Risk, disorder, and adap*tation (pp. 72–95). New York: John Wiley.

Saltzman, W. R., Steinberg, A. M., Layne, C. M., Aisenberg, E., & Pynoos, R. S. (2001). A developmental approach to school-based treatment of adolescents exposed to trauma and traumatic loss. *Journal of Child and Adolescent Group Therapy, 11,* 43–56.

Schwab-Stone, M. E., Chen, C., Greenberger, E., Silver, D., Lichtman, J., & Voyce, C. (1999). No safe haven II: The effects of violence exposure on urban youth. *Journal of the American Academy of Child and Adolescent Psychiatry, 38,* 359–367.

Widom, C. S. (1999). Posttraumatic stress disorder in abused and neglected children grown up. *American Journal of Psychiatry, 156,* 1223–1229.

15

Children
During Wartime

Robert A. Murphy

Children displaced by political conflict and war suffer the most severe disruptions to healthy development along the six pathways, and are at highest risk for posttrauma stress disorders. Their parents and caregivers often are limited in their ability to help the children because of their own exposure to the traumas of war, and a family's history of wartime adversity may be compounded by an uncertain legal status within their country of refuge. Mental health professionals who are knowledgeable about child trauma and the sequelae of war can help teachers understand their students' urgent psychological needs, language and learning deficits, and health concerns, which must be addressed alongside broader issues of children's psychological and social adaptation within their schools, families, and communities.

Warfare and mass violence disproportionately affect women and children throughout the world (Yule, 2000). In the early 1900s, children constituted approximately five percent of those injured and killed during war. By World War II, they accounted for 65 percent; in recent wars this figure has risen to 90 percent of injuries and casualties (Save the Children, 2002). Surviving children are subject to tremendous disruption during critical periods of development. There are more than eight million children worldwide who are refugees of war (Malakoff, 1994), and many more are displaced within and outside their home countries due to political, economic, or ethnic persecution. The vast majority of wars occur in developing countries, where combat compounds the widespread effects of abject poverty (Save the Children, 2002).

MODERN WARFARE
AND ITS REFUGEES

Warfare is historically defined as an armed conflict carried out under government direction where civilians are not the primary targets of violence. Modern warfare has extended well beyond this definition to become a chronic conflict in which civilians, including children, are systematic targets of violence. Similarly, when children and families must anticipate constant threat, assumptions about public unity in support of a common wartime goal as a mediating factor in the development of posttraumatic symptoms may no longer apply. Wars no longer pit one army against another, but instead are focused on the destruction of an "enemy" society through the systematic destruction of homes, food and water supplies, and families; the latter occurs through physical and sexual violence perpetrated against women and children (Save the Children, 2002).

Initial waves of refugees tend to come from economically or educationally advantaged groups with the means to escape their adversity and travel to a more benign locale or country. As war expands and affects a broader swath of families, those with fewer resources make up subsequent waves of émigrés, arriving in their new homelands with long histories of economic and social adversity. They may have been exposed directly as victims or indirectly as witnesses to severe violence, torture, and trauma, perhaps inflicted upon parents, siblings, or other loved ones. At a time of maximum reliance on their caregivers for security and safety, child victims and witnesses are cared for by adults who are themselves overwhelmed with terror and panic in the face of gunfire, bombings, injury, and death. Some youngsters are forced into service as child soldiers and thus become perpetrators of violence (Save the Children, 2002). Still others arrive in their new country of residence after long and arduous journeys marked by extended stays in detention centers and camps where basic nutrition, hygiene, education, and income are severely restricted.

War disrupts the basic prerequisites for adequate child development; a predictable environment and secure caregiving are shattered. Basic psychological needs may go unmet due to understandable preoccupations aroused by the lack of food, shelter, and for children, education. Caregivers become limited in their capacity to respond to their children's needs as a result of their own experiences of trauma. Loss represents a prototypical experience for children who endure wartime conditions. Children can be forcefully separated from other family members and forced to migrate to distant regions under the threat of injury, starvation, and death. Many have lost important loved ones, perhaps in terrifying and horrendous ways. For these children, their survival and relocation heralds newfound safety, but is complicated by departure from a familiar society and culture and, perhaps, feelings of guilt or remorse related to earlier losses and actions.

Children can be exposed to the conditions of war for extended periods of time, often living in fear for their lives and the lives of loved ones and, in the aftermath, exposed to repeated and grotesque reminders in the form of shattered buildings and dead or mutilated bodies (Laor & Wolmer, 2002; Yule, 2000). As with many other types of psychological problems, girls who experience war appear more prone to internalizing symptoms (e.g., depression, anxiety, physical complaints) and boys to externalizing symptoms (e.g., disruptive behavior, attention problems). Those more likely to experience significant emotional disturbance related to wartime experiences, include those for whom war does not represent their first experiences of adversity or trauma, as well as those who lack the consistent support of parents or other adult caregivers.

In the longer term, children who have experienced war are themselves at risk for serious mental health problems, including posttraumatic stress disorder, depression, anxiety and fearfulness, substance abuse, interpersonal problems, and difficulty with self-regulation and behavior control (Lustig et al., 2002). Presentation varies widely among those children who become symptomatic. Symptoms tend to wax and wane over time and may not become apparent for many years. Younger children, by virtue of their day-to-day reliance on their parents or other caregivers, are most influenced by the extent to which war disrupts parental functioning and environmental stability. Older children, in contrast, tend to be more affected by the reactions and responses of their peers (Laor, Wolmer, & Adessky, 2000; Laor et al., 1997).

Many children continue to experience serious symptoms well into adulthood (Sack, Him, & Dickason, 1999). From an outside perspective, some may appear well adjusted, succeeding in school or work, yet they may still experience significant problems with anxiety, depression, or interpersonal relationships (Laor & Wolmer, 2002; Sack et al., 1999).

TEACHING THE CHILDREN OF WAR

Upon arrival in their new countries of residence, children of war are ill equipped to succeed in unfamiliar educational settings. Many have missed crucial periods of learning and lack basic skills related to language and mathematics. Learning deficits may be compounded by emotional distress related both to wartime experiences and to the stress of resettlement in an unfamiliar land. Parents and caregivers may themselves lack educational skills; language barriers and illiteracy impede their participation in their children's schooling.

A history of wartime adversity may be compounded by an uncertain legal status within their country of refuge. For example, more than 50 percent of refugee children from South America living in the United States have experienced war-related trauma and have entered the United States without legal protection. As a result, these children may be unable to access basic and necessary medical and mental health care.

Despite recognition of the potentially enduring effects of children's exposure to war, few education and mental health professionals have sufficient training and preparation to respond to the myriad challenges presented by these children. Educators in particular may feel burdened by unrealistic expectations about overcoming the damages inflicted by wartime experiences.

More realistically, educators would benefit from an awareness of the nature of children's wartime experiences, the developmental needs of such children, their common reactions, and the range of symptoms they may display. When teachers consult and collaborate with mental health professionals who are knowledgeable about child trauma and the sequelae of war, teachers' understanding increases. This understanding assists them in their primary educational mission. For example, children who have been persecuted or witnessed persecution of their loved ones may be suspicious of authority figures. Because schools in some countries became systematic targets of violence, children may struggle to adapt or may actively resist some of the routines and rules of the school setting and be reluctant to confide in educators who have the best intentions (Yule, 2000).

The engagement through school of children affected by war can be crucial to restoring a sense of predictability and stability in their lives, as well as teaching valuable academic and life survival skills. Many of the principles that apply to the success of education in general are especially relevant to immigrant and refugee children. Given their experiences of overwhelming adversity, children who have experienced war-related trauma require particular attention from educators who are dedicated to forming supportive and mentoring relationships and fostering achievement in their students (Suarez-Orozco, 2001).

An emphasis on the social climate of a school complements the academic strivings of many refugee and immigrant families and should enhance their engagement (Comer, Ben-Avie, Haynes, & Joyner, 1999; Group for the Advancement of Psychiatry Committee on Preventive Psychiatry, 1999). From this perspective, mental health concerns can be addressed alongside broader issues of children's psychological and social adaptation within their schools, families, and communities.

REFERENCES

Comer, J. P., Ben-Avie, M., Haynes, N. M., & Joyner, E. T. (Eds.). (1999). *Child by child: The Comer process for change in education.* New York: Teachers College Press.

Group for the Advancement of Psychiatry Committee on Preventive Psychiatry. (1999). Violent behavior in children and youth: Preventive intervention from a psychiatric perspective. *Journal of the American Academy of Child and Adolescent Psychiatry, 38,* 235–241.

Laor, N., & Wolmer, L. (2002). Children exposed to disaster: The role of the mental health professional. In M. Lewis (Ed.), *Child and adolescent psychiatry: A comprehensive textbook* (3rd ed., pp. 925–937). Baltimore, MD: Lippincott Williams & Wilkins.

Laor, N., Wolmer, L., & Adessky, R. S. (2000). *A short-term model of individual therapy for children and adults following a trauma.* Tel-Aviv: Tel-Aviv Trauma Center.

Laor, N., Wolmer, L., Mayes, L. C., Wiezman, R., Gershon, A., & Cohen, D. J. (1997). Israeli preschool children under SCUDs: A 30-month follow-up. *Journal of the American Academy of Child and Adolescent Psychiatry, 36,* 349–356.

Lustig, S. L., Kia-Keating, M., Knight, W. G., Geltman, P., Ellis, H., Keane, T., & Saxe, G. N. (2002). *White paper: Child and adolescent refugee mental health.* Boston: National Child Traumatic Stress Network and Center for Medical and Refugee Trauma.

Malakoff, M. E. (1994). Refugee children and violence. In C. Chiland & J. G. Young (Eds.), *Children and violence* (pp. 145–159). Northvale, NJ: Jason Aronson.

Sack, W. H., Him, C., & Dickason, D. M. (1999). Twelve-year follow-up study of Khmer youths who suffered massive war trauma as children. *Journal of the American Academy of Child & Adolescent Psychiatry, 38,* 1173–1179.

Save the Children. (2002). *State of the world's mothers: Mothers and children in war and conflict.* Westport, CT: Author.

Suarez-Orozco, C. (2001). Understanding and serving the children of immigrants. *Harvard Educational Review, 71,* 579–589.

Yule, W. (2000). From pogroms to "ethnic cleansing": Meeting the needs of war affected children. *Journal of Child Psychology, Psychiatry and Allied Disciplines, 41,* 695–702.

16

Children of the World

How We Created a Full-Service School

Grace Nebb

The Comer Process encourages powerful partnerships that extend beyond the school walls. The principal of a formerly deprived and neglected Florida elementary school with a largely poor, immigrant population describes the school's transformation through partnerships with parents, foundations, universities, social and health service organizations, and government and civic organizations. Now an exemplar of community mobilization and empowerment, the school embraces even its future students—literally from birth—in an environment that provides stability, hope, and skills.

DAILY CRISIS MANAGEMENT

I was the principal of Fienberg/Fisher Elementary School, one of the most deprived and neglected schools in the area of South Beach, Miami, Florida. Our population was composed of poor immigrant families from all over the globe, most of them Hispanic, and many of them refugees from countries at war.

Forty-five different nationalities were represented in our student body. Ninety-three percent were on free or reduced-price lunch, 50 percent were LEP (Limited English Proficient) students, and—aggravating our situation—our mobility rate was 54 percent. The area where the school was located was a haven for drug dealers and criminals. Since our campus was not fenced in, these individuals roamed the school at night and in the early morning hours.

From 1987 to 1991 I was the school's assistant principal. In 1992, the year we started implementing the Comer Process, I was promoted to principal and served at Fienberg/Fisher until 2000. As the assistant principal, I spent my days trying to deal with safety concerns, overwhelming academic deficiencies, acute absenteeism, low morale and expectations from staff, and no parental support. I felt myself reacting to daily crises with little time left for planning or reflection.

With support from Florida International University and a $60,000 grant from the Danforth Foundation, our school had the opportunity to embark on a reform adventure that would transform the entire school community. The goal was to create the conditions needed to develop a full-service school through community mobilization and empowerment. We named it "The Healthy Learners Program."

CREATING THE HEALTHY LEARNERS PROGRAM

After meeting several times with the university and foundation coordinators, we decided to hire a full-time social worker who would begin working with the community. We conducted a door-to-door community needs assessment and discovered that our parents, although poor and with little educational background, had tremendous survival skills and strengths. All wished their children success in school, and they were willing to help—"if only we knew how."

The survey indicated the following problems and needs:

- feelings of isolation and a lack of support groups
- a "one-stop shop" to access social, medical, and mental health services
- affordable housing (the area was being gentrified, and many families were being evicted from their tiny efficiencies)
- affordable child care
- homework assistance for their children, including a quiet place to complete homework

In the next step, we brought the parents into the school. We met in parking lots, in the Children of the World Park (located between school buildings), in the hallways, and outside the office. We visited their homes, and waited for them in the morning when they dropped off their children and in the afternoon during pick-up time. We invited small groups to the school for coffee and cookies on a daily basis.

During this time, the program coordinator and the social worker were in the process of developing a parent-training component. They created a 40-hour module divided into 20 hours of class work (learning interviewing techniques, community outreach, school rules and procedures, understanding agencies' criteria for accessing services, availability of services, filling out forms, and much more) and 20 hours in the field (visiting families and social, health, and mental health agencies; and meeting with the administrative staff). Finally, a committed group of 10 parents became the first participants in the program. The grant provided a small incentive: $40 at the completion of the module.

RAIN (REFERRAL AND INFORMATION NETWORK) IS BORN

The training opened new horizons for this once-isolated group of moms. Through the expert coaching provided by the social worker, the parents decided to begin working on the first two identified needs:

- Create a support group for other parents.
- Create the one-stop shop to provide information and access to services.

They all agreed on the name Referral and Information Network (RAIN) as their name. When I asked them the reason for choosing that name, they answered, "We will provide a shower of services to our children and their families."

After several months of preparation, and meetings with service providers and school officials, the moms were ready to launch a campaign of family advocacy and empowerment, high expectations, and hope. Building the foundation of our village had just begun.

During the first year, my role was to support, learn, and listen. I managed to provide a classroom, which became the RAIN Room. We added partitions to create small offices. A phone/fax line was connected, and a computer and printer were borrowed from our existing computer lab. In another section of the room, a family center welcomed families in need of support, or just looking for a place to sit and chat for a while about common concerns. The Rainmakers, as they were fondly called by all, began providing the much-needed services. They became experts at referring and connecting families to the right agencies. They became case managers, and the RAIN Room was the first office to be visited by families who were new to the country.

By the end of the school year, the social worker managed to set up several service providers at the school. These providers were assigned by their agencies to perform their services at the school. Then we realized we had made our first mistake: While some agencies had too many customers to handle, others sat unoccupied all day long. We realized that in our eagerness to find services, we had overlooked the most important aspect of our program—to include our parents in the selection of the services to be provided.

To ensure their involvement in the process a consortium of parents; social, mental health, and health agency administrators; city officials; leaders of community organizations; and school staff was formed. The Healthy Learners Consortium met in the school's media center on a monthly basis. With support and guidance from the social worker and the school staff, the parents prepared agendas, mailed invitations and minutes to the community, contacted the news media, and chaired their meetings.

Initially, the meetings were not well attended and there was no follow-up. Agency representatives would come and go without committing their services to the school. There was no communication among stakeholders, and little interest was generated. The few services we offered were not integrated and in most cases were duplicated by our own staff and other outside agencies. We had no established procedures for referrals to service providers and no monitoring of students' progress. The staff complained about how much time elapsed between Child Study Team meetings, their lack of understanding regarding the referred child's problems, and the inadequacy of the support and communication provided to them.

The following year, 1992, I was appointed principal of the school. At that time, the district was offering a menu of researched-based programs that Title I schools could select from and implement. The School Development Program seemed to offer the organizational framework we needed to make all the pieces fit together. The vote was almost unanimous. Staff and parent training began immediately. The Comer Process was introduced to everyone and embraced by all. The program focused our school on a more successful path while building trust among staff, parents, and service providers, and a positive can-do attitude among all. The integration of the full-service component into the school and community was on its way.

The Child Study Team was reorganized into the Student and Staff Support Team (SSST). Originally, this team had been composed of a social worker who was assigned to our school three times per week, a full-time counselor, one administrator, and the referring teacher. Parents were invited to these meetings but seldom attended. The meetings were conducted with the general expectation of a referral for a psychological evaluation and a placement in an exceptional education program (ESE).

A fresh new outlook with a developmental approach was initiated. We reviewed and redesigned roles. We clarified procedures and, most important, changed attitudes and expectations.

The school social worker had a master's degree (M.S.W.), but her main duties consisted of verifying students' addresses and completing social histories. After much deliberation, we decided to reassign the address verifications to the Rainmakers. This would permit the social worker's inclusion as an integral member of the SSST. At the same time, the Rainmakers benefited from these home visits by announcing and offering their services to the community in a more personal manner.

We convinced the school psychologist, who was assigned to the school twice per week, to participate in the team meetings. Her developmental perspective and specific suggestions to redirect behaviors became powerful tools in preventing potential problems. The counselor, who was bombarded with paperwork, delegated some of her responsibilities to our clerical staff. This allowed her to do what she did best: work with individual and small groups of students, make presentations to staff regarding accommodations and alternative strategies to be implemented in the classrooms, provide consultation to teachers regarding the six developmental pathways and classroom practice, and meet with our families. She became the cochair and the liaison between the staff and the SSST.

An English for Speakers of Other Languages (ESOL) teacher was added to the team. Since 50 percent of our population was composed of LEP students, her input and suggestions were invaluable. She provided the team with greater insight and understanding regarding our students' linguistic and cultural challenges. This once shy and quiet individual developed into a fierce and vocal advocate for our immigrant families.

One of our exceptional education teachers brought to the SSST expert recommendations and demonstrations regarding special accommodations, different approaches to curriculum delivery, and viable solutions to once seemingly impossible situations. Her schedule was creatively modified, and she was provided support to enable her participation in the team. Both our ESOL and Exceptional Education Program teachers gave inservice training with meaningful hands-on workshops to other staff members. Topics varied from cultural understanding of students and families from all of South America, Central America, and the Caribbean Islands to the implementation of a child-centered classroom.

Teachers or parents initiated all referrals by filling out a prereferral form. The program coordinator (social worker), who became the team chairperson, coordinated the process from beginning to end. She made all referrals to the service providers as needed and monitored each child's progress. She ensured that all referring teachers and parents received information regarding the student's progress. She kept the lines of communication open between the service providers and the school. By creating a universal Consent to Share Information form that was signed by the parents, counselors and therapists were able to participate in multiagency team meetings. Team members who worked with a particular student shared pertinent information with each other in an attempt to improve the child's outcome. In this way, all efforts were integrated and coordinated. The three guiding principles of no-fault, consensus, and collaboration contributed to the development of trust and respect among all stakeholders. Turf issues that initially plagued our meetings and slowed down our progress became a thing of the past. It is important to emphasize that the social worker position was originally funded by a grant from the Danforth Foundation. Before the grant ended, everyone realized the importance of this position. After meeting with the School Planning and Management Team (SPMT), it was unanimously decided by consensus to institutionalize it by allocating Title I funds.

All SSST members became case managers. Our jobs were to observe the child in different learning and social situations in order to provide feedback to the team and the teacher, to contact the family, and to develop the trust needed to work as a unit toward common goals. To ensure every child's healthy learning and to strengthen families, we also kept in touch with the service providers and reported the child's progress to the team. Weekly meetings were scheduled with the assistance of the Rainmakers. They contacted the parents and explained the importance of these meetings. Parent participation in the meetings improved dramatically. Now these meetings were no longer a "study in hopelessness." They had become meaningful conversations about solutions.

Communication among teams was accomplished by the participation of several members of the SSST in the SPMT (which is called the Educational Excellence School Advisory Council [EESAC] in Miami-Dade County). This back-and-forth communication allowed the SSST to address global issues, work on preventive strategies, and understand the roots of the problems. No longer did we look the other way and hope for the best. Now we had a team of professionals and well-trained parents who could provide immediate assistance to families in crisis and who could support our staff.

The Healthy Learners Consortium took a new turn as well. This grassroots effort led by parents became an impressive and persistent voice that spoke on behalf of our children and their families. By pointing out specific community-related concerns, suggesting possible solutions, and avoiding the "blaming game," many battles were fought and won at these meetings. Persistent problems that seemed impossible to resolve were tackled effectively by this powerful organization. Regular representation from city officials, the office of the mayor, and law enforcement officials became a monthly occurrence. Several organizations joined as active members: The Miami Beach Development Corporation, Miami Beach Housing Authority, Legal Services of Greater Miami, Stanley Myers Clinic, Boys and Girls Club, Children's Psychiatric Center, Jewish Family Services, Department of Children and Families, and others. Florida International University, Barry University, and the University of Miami provided professional and technical assistance to the parents and the school. They were instrumental in the school's receiving awards and grants.

HOME INTERVENTION TEAMS

As the Comer Process began to change the climate of the entire school community, our staff became eager to implement new techniques that would improve their students' academic gains. A general concern from staff was the students' poor attendance. Although we tried different incentive initiatives, none were truly successful. It was agreed that the SSST would investigate the main causes of this pervasive problem and make recommendations to improve it. A meeting that included the Rainmakers took place. Reports of individual classroom attendance were duplicated and distributed to each member of the team. Those students with severe attendance problems were noted and discussed. Since many of our parents did not have phones, the only way to contact them was through home visits or waiting for them at dismissal time. We did both. Soon we discovered the reasons for so many absences: *Lice*. Many of our families did not know how to get rid of this nuisance and did not have the money to buy the product needed to eliminate it. In some cases the epidemic was so pervasive among family members that even the babies needed treatment. The Rainmakers decided to create the Lice Busters Campaign. They developed a family training component to eradicate lice throughout the household. Videotapes, flyers, and supplies were purchased. The social worker requested assistance from the neighborhood clinic to donate the lice shampoo. Kits containing laundry detergent, plastic bags, and small, fine-tooth combs were distributed to the families along with specific instructions explaining how to get rid of lice in the bedding, carpets, and elsewhere. We found that most of our families applied the shampoo to their children but failed to wash the sheets and vacuum their carpets. Lice came back almost immediately. We also discovered that many families did not own a vacuum cleaner, so it was very difficult to remove lice from the carpets. Again, the Rainmakers provided us with a wonderful solution: They offered their services upon request to vacuum the lice-infested carpets. Their campaign was so effective that the local newspapers covered their story. Soon our attendance improved and the campaign was duplicated in schools across the Miami Beach area.

THE HOMEWORK CLUB

It was during an SPMT meeting that problems with homework became a school priority. Assistance was requested from the SSST to begin to unravel root causes of these problems. A meeting was scheduled and the Rainmakers were invited to attend. We discovered that most families lived in crowded studio apartments and that appropriate space to do homework was unavailable. Through the community needs assessment, we also found out that many parents requested assistance in providing adequate space for their children to complete their homework. The Rainmakers volunteered their services and began working with small groups of children after school. They became so successful working with the children that in one month the number of students increased from 20 to 100. The Homework Club initiative was introduced to the Healthy Learners Consortium in hope of gaining support from one of the agencies. The Boys and Girls Club, which was already providing afterschool sports to our students, responded to the increasing need to serve more students and provided funding for four teachers to assist the Rainmakers. Each teacher worked in collaboration with two Rainmakers. They planned their activities together and grouped the students by grade levels. The program was conducted from Monday through Thursday for one hour after school. This was the first time I witnessed our teachers and parents working together for a common goal!

HEAD START INITIATIVE

As the parents became well-informed, active community members, they began to earn everyone's respect and admiration. It was becoming easier to solicit services and resources for the school. One example was Head Start. During a consortium meeting, one of our parents explained that the families had a general concern about not being able to offer meaningful preschool experiences to their children. She expressed the importance of engaging very young children's minds and beginning their immersion in positive social, developmental, and educational activities as early as possible. Even though our school had three pre-K classes, everyone felt that it would be to our students' advantage to begin their training at age three. It was no coincidence that the Community Action Agency director, who was an active member of the Healthy Learners Consortium, was searching for a place to install two portable buildings, each of which would house two Head Start classrooms! After securing the necessary approvals from regional and district superintendents, Head Start became an integral part of our school program. The program offered highly trained teachers; fully furnished, brand-new portable buildings; and materials. Our district provided the land, installation services, and inclusion in our school lunch program. Head Start took care of the rest.

After the first year we could see the difference in the children's readiness level when they entered our pre-K program at age four. By the time they entered kindergarten at age five they were ready for the world! This is just one example of what a group of well-informed, "Comerized" parents was able to establish at the school.

THE CHILDREN OF
THE WORLD HEALTH CENTER

As the Healthy Learners Program continued to grow, services and providers were added to the RAIN Room. Our collaborations with the community flourished. It was evident that lack of adequate space was becoming our biggest concern. The social worker researched the availability of grants. She discovered state Public Education Capital Outlay (PECO) funds designated to construct buildings/relocatables that could house full-service programs at schools. After securing approval and support from our region, our work began. The state awarded $750,000 to construct a 4,500-square-foot relocatable building that would house our entire full-service program.

Finally, after almost two years of battling the bureaucracy, our dream became a reality. The Children of the World Health Center opened its doors to our school community. The Stanley C. Myers Community Health Center hired a nurse practitioner, a nurse assistant, and a part-time clerk who would provide medical services free of charge. They also provided the medical equipment and supplies. The University of Miami offered the services of a doctor who consulted with patients at least two times per week, and the placement of several medical interns who were supervised by both the nurse practitioner and the doctor. The School of Social Work at Barry

University placed several social work interns under the supervision of our social worker; these interns provided individual, group, and family counseling and participated as case managers in our SSST meetings.

The center also housed other service providers who were highly committed to strengthening and assisting our children and their families. The RAIN Room now constituted a large wing of offices beautifully furnished and fully equipped with computers, copy machines, faxes, and phones. A large area was dedicated to the Bright Horizons Room, a parent resource room fully equipped with several computers and checkout materials. Parent breakfast meetings and training sessions were held in that room. Another large area was dedicated to the future Raindrop Center. This would become an affordable child care center managed and operated by the Rainmakers.

The participation of these agencies was a direct result of an entire year of dialogue and planning among the SPMT, which brought the global issues to the table; the SSST, which investigated and developed an understanding of the root causes of problems and possible solutions; the Rainmakers, who provided the most important perspectives and insights of all, and involved and mobilized the entire community; and the Healthy Learners Consortium, which met month after month with all the service providers, city and school officials, and the parents in an attempt to provide these much-needed services to a community in crisis.

COOL SCHOOL

South Beach is a haven for gangs and drug dealers. Some of the night custodians noticed that a group of about seven to nine kids was hanging around the school late at night. Evidence of their presence was left in the form of beer bottles and trash strewn all over the Children of the World Park.

One night the social worker and I decided to confront these youngsters. Surprisingly, they were all very young, no more than 16 years of age. Some of them knew who I was. They had been our own students! This reality was extremely disturbing to both the social worker and me. Where did we go wrong? What happened to these children between elementary school and high school? After a while, we established some rapport with them and asked them the same questions. Their answers were honest and to the point.

They wished they had a place to go after school where they could just hang out with their friends and have a good time without getting into trouble. Most of these children went to empty homes after school. They spent too much time alone, or with inappropriate company, and lacked guidance. We had to reexamine what was currently being offered to our students. The school already provided the Homework Club, an academic excellence program, and the Boys and Girls Club operated a sports program. All were good afterschool programs. None, however, worked on gang prevention or on developing positive self-images. None seemed to address the needs identified by our former students.

We decided to create such a place. With the assistance of Florida International University, we submitted a proposal to the state with all the new ideas represented. In 1995 the school was awarded the amount of $250,000 to implement Cool School, a therapeutic afterschool program for students in Grades Three through Six. Our goal was to provide a safe environment where children could develop self-esteem and positive self-images. Cool School operated five days per week and served children who were identified as being at risk. The program served 80 children ages seven to 13 and was staffed by social workers, teachers, paraprofessionals, and volunteers. Cool School operated in collaboration with the Miami Beach Police Department's Gang Resistance, Education and Treatment (GREAT) program. The uniqueness of the program was its focus on prevention instead of intervention. Children chose from a variety of scheduled activities that included: academic enhancement, gang prevention, substance abuse prevention, sports, computer instruction, fine and applied arts, field trips, and group counseling. In addition, monthly parent meetings were a requirement for participation in the program. Cool School was in operation for five years (1995–2000). The grant monies were "stretched" for two years but we needed additional resources to continue its operation. The social worker came up with the idea of incorporating Cool School. This allowed us to compete for block grants and develop new partnerships. The City of Miami Beach, United Way of Miami-Dade, the Miami Beach and Miami Police Departments, United Health Care of Florida, Boys and Girls Club of Miami, Florida International University, Florida State University, Barry University, University of Miami, Miami-Dade County Transit, Stanley Myers Community Health Center, Miami Heat, and HIP of Florida became our new allies.

Cool School received numerous awards and accolades. Among the most notable were the following:

- Miami-Dade Partners Exemplary Award Honorable Mention—1998–1999
- National Children's Film Festival—Second Place Elementary School Division Feature Film—*Detention Bytes*, 1998
- Presenter at the Governor's Third Annual Children's Summit—1998
- Presenter at the Seventh Annual Children's Mental Health Conference, Linking Forces VII, *Cool School: A Therapeutic After School Program*—1998
- Presenter at the National Youth Crime Prevention Conference—1997
- Miami-Dade Partners Award for Joint Venture—1997
- Miami-Dade Partners Award for Community Service—1996
- Miami Beach Development Corporation Award for Community Service—1996

Presentations were made by our social worker, Allison Tomchin, and some of the Cool School participants.

Cool School took the afterschool program concept to new heights. "Get out and learn the world" was a focus of this results-oriented program. Participating students' records indicated improved attendance, grades, and overall attitudes and feelings toward school and themselves. The best indicator of the success of this program was our alumni returning to our school to volunteer at Cool School.

An emphasis on attentive and consistent relationships with students and staff underlay the Cool School approach. The bottom line was that staff must be positive and nonjudgmental. The program was designed to provide positive role models, guidance, and support to all in a safe, no-fault environment.

THE RAINDROP CENTER

Another major goal identified by the community was affordable child care. After five years of planning, Raindrop opened its doors to the school community.

Currently, Dade's schools have child care centers at more than 14 public high schools, six vocational/adult education facilities, and two alternative education schools. Unlike the other child care centers, where high school and adult education students receive hands-on training, Raindrop is not run by the school district, though the district supplied the building, furniture, equipment, and maintenance. The Rainmakers became state-certified in child care, and staffed Raindrop. As the grant money inevitably ran out, the social worker offered different opportunities to the Rainmakers that would generate sufficient funds to continue their project. One was to become an incorporated nonprofit organization. This status enabled them to compete for block grants and other means to support their program. The Rainmakers transformed into RAIN Parents, Inc. They applied for and received several grants from different organizations such as the United Way, Bell South, the City of Miami Beach, and others. The Raindrop Center housed 21 babies and toddlers in a rich, child-centered environment. RAIN charged $75 per week to those who could afford it and provided vouchers to those who qualified for them. To keep themselves abreast of the latest techniques in child development and school readiness, they hired a coordinator who provided training opportunities and managed their grants. In addition, our pre-K teachers volunteered to assist the moms in hands-on training related to the preschool curriculum and child development activities. The teachers often visited the child care center, modeled lessons, and invited the Rainmakers to observe their teaching. The Raindrop babies were invited to our programs and assemblies, they visited the pre-K and Head Start classrooms, and were included in our lunch program. Some of the upper-grade teachers participated in a Buddy Reading program, and on many occasions fifth- and sixth-grade students were invited to read stories to the group. It was a win-win situation.

> From a once-neglected and unsuccessful school to a national model for community mobilization and empowerment, our school broke every possible predictable statistical record that was based on high risk, poverty, and mobility. The Florida Accountability System awarded the school a grade of "A" during the 1999–2000 school year.

A school environment where creativity, risk taking, respect, and personal development are cherished and fostered was many years in the making. From a once-neglected and unsuccessful school to a national model for community mobilization and empowerment, our school broke every possible predictable statistical record that was based on high risk, poverty, and mobility. The Florida Accountability System awarded the school a grade of "A" during the 1999–2000 school year.

The organizational framework provided by the Comer Process assisted us in making sense of an extremely complex idea. SDP taught us how to ensure integration, communication, and follow-up procedures among all stakeholders; how to create the conditions to make good development and learning possible for all our students as well as our staff and parents; and how to build and maintain positive interpersonal relationships and trust.

Index

NOTE: Page numbers in *italic* type refer to figures, tables, or boxes.

**CORWIN
PRESS**